The Fall of the Church

The Fall of the Church

ROGER HAYDON MITCHELL

WIPF & STOCK · Eugene, Oregon

THE FALL OF THE CHURCH

Wipf & Stock
An Imprint of Wipf and Stock Publishers
199 W. 8th Ave., Suite 3
Eugene, OR 97401
www.wipfandstock.com

ISBN 13: 978-1-62032-928-3
Manufactured in the U.S.A.

Contents

Preface

WHO'S THIS BOOK FOR?

THIS BOOK IS PRIMARILY intended for those, like me, who are motivated by love for people and the world and are troubled by the increasing commodification that reduces work, leisure, art, education, and human relationships in general to a market value. It is for those who, when looking for the spiritual resources for radical love in the face of its opposite, find this kind of love consummately expressed in the character and life of Jesus as portrayed in the gospel narratives. Many of us, while recognizing that the story of Jesus meets our contemporary desire, find a constant tension between Jesus and the largely hierarchically controlled, legalistically orientated, temple-centered organization of the church. While the book is aimed at many of us from the Christian mainstream who embrace Jesus' kind of love as the way to live but struggle hugely with the tension to the point of deliberate or involuntary exile from the church, these are emphatically not its only concern. It also has in mind those agnostics, members of other faith groups, neo-Marxists, and humanists who are attracted to Jesus but have likewise found the contradiction between his way of life and the associated hierarchical system of law and temple a serious obstacle to taking his life and teaching seriously.

THE BOOK'S AIM AND PURPOSE

The book explores the roots of this tension between the loving Jesus and the often oppressive behavior of the church in order to provide a lens and a language with which better to see, hear, and interpret the deep story of the Western world. The hope is to provide tools with which the reader will be more able to understand and reflect on what is happening in our contemporary culture and society. In order to keep the book relatively short, those who want access to the detailed research behind the arguments are encouraged to pursue the references given, and in particular the thesis set out in the earlier academic work *Church, Gospel, & Empire: How the Politics of Sovereignty Impregnated the West*. I spent the best part of six years doing the academic research for that previous book, and almost a lifetime of practical preparation. Nevertheless, the end result, while well received and endorsed, was necessarily somewhat technical, and, as many of my friends have told me, needed constant reference to a good dictionary to decipher! This book aims to make what my copy editor has described as "life-giving truth" more accessible while at the same time going significantly further in exposing and applying its contemporary implications.

There are six interrelated objectives that have guided the eventual form and content of this book. The first is to show how the historical alignment of Christianity with the dominant law-hierarchy-temple system and the consequent displacement of Jesus helps account for the contemporary conundrum of the sense of marginalization felt by both Christian and secular people. The second separates out two conflicting streams in Christianity: the love stream which the stories of Jesus portray, and the sovereignty system that much of the theology, ecclesiology, and mission of the church represents. Thirdly, it attempts to explain briefly and succinctly how these two streams arose in the early stages of Western history. Fourthly, its purpose is to demonstrate that far from being two partly complementary, or at least alternative expressions of Christianity, the sovereignty stream embodies the very system of governance that the gospel story shows Jesus opposing and bringing to an end. Fifthly, it makes clear from the story of Jesus in the context of its Hebrew history and Gentile Greco-Roman present that, rather than confronting the empire system in its own violent, dominating spirit, God has remained within the church and the empire in order to empty out the domination system from the inside. This is how God has worked in the cycles of history, consistent with the way that God stayed with Israel and its neighboring imperial powers during the fall of the Jews. The book indicates that this divine strategy continued with the fall of the church and is coming to a head, right now, in our contemporary Western world. Finally, the purpose of the book is to prepare the ground for the emergence and practice of kenarchy: the humanity-loving, world-embracing, inclusive approach to life and the universe introduced and explored in the soon-following companion volume *Discovering Kenarchy*.

HOW THE BOOK SETS ABOUT THESE OBJECTIVES

The book is arranged over five chapters. The first unpacks the background to the already mentioned conundrum of why both Christian and secular people feel similarly marginalized yet perceive the other to be in the position of greater power. Chapter 2 begins to tell the story of what I discovered from my four investigative case studies. It sets out the way that the exercise of sovereign power came to be seen as the means to peace for humankind from its beginnings in the days of the early church historian Eusebius and his partnership with the emperor Constantine. It explores the operation of sovereignty in the conflict and division of the authorities of church and empire throughout the Middle Ages after the fall of Rome, and it traces the progress of the Christendom system in the multiplication and diversification of sovereign power through war, law, and money. It culminates in explaining the modern rationalistic rejection of transcendence as the carrier of universal sovereign rule. Chapter 3 briefly relates the history of the love stream as it paralleled the partnership of church and empire, examining how and why it so easily defaulted to the domination system. Chapter 4 then explains how war, law, and money, identified as the currencies of sovereignty, are coming together in a present-day fullness that political philosophers and analysts call biopower. I suggest that the Holy Spirit is both on the inside and outside of this system; within, in what the neo-Marxists call the potential power of immaterial labor, and on the outside, in the egalitarian grace of Pentecostal outpouring, terms which the chapter carefully unpacks. The chapter explains how these two factors might activate the seismic shift in the Western mindset necessary to break free from the sovereignty system at last. Finally Chapter 5 addresses some of the most resistant obstacles to the repentance required if we are more completely to engage the contemporary world with radical love.

Acknowledgments

FIRST OF ALL I thank Richard Roberts, Professor Emeritus of Religious Studies at Lancaster University and Visiting Emeritus Professor in the Division of Languages and Religion at the University of Stirling, Graham Ward, Regius Professor of Divinity at the University of Oxford, Arthur Bradley, Reader in the Department of English and Creative Writing at Lancaster University, and Ray Mayhew of the Dubai Centre for Prayer and Biblical Studies for their endorsements of my previous academic book, *Church, Gospel, & Empire: How the Gospel of Sovereignty Impregnated the West.* Their affirmation encouraged me to attempt this more popular version of the perspectives set out there. Secondly, because I believe that all knowledge is relational and that we never truly understand anything alone, I am particularly grateful to those who have worked with me on this book, reading each chapter and commenting on both the language and content and recommending corrections and changes that have made this a better book than it would otherwise have been. For this labor of love I thank first of all my wife and fellow subversive Sue Mitchell, together with my good friends Dr Andy Knox, Mike Love, and Julie Tomlin. Although I am wholeheartedly committed to collaboration I am not always very good at it, and have not always received their advice with the grace I would have liked to display! Then there are those many supporters in prayer and love, especially fellow kenarchists Michael Lafleur and Sam Cooper of Mississauga, Canada, Martin and Gayle Scott of Cadiz, Spain, and Stephen Rusk and Peter McKinney of Northern Ireland, as well as our trustees Dr Mike Winter, Keith and Suzy Wilkinson, and Angela Prestwich, whose practical help and faithfulness over many years cannot go unrecorded. I must mention my wonderful continental friends, Sam and Michelle Rhein of Nice, France and Michael and Andrea Schiffmann of Hanover, Germany, whose input into my life and thought has been immeasurable. Finally I am once again indebted to Sandy Waldron, my indefatigable copy editor, whose careful partnership has brought this book to publication.

1

A Contemporary Conundrum

(A) INTRODUCTION: SETTING OUT THE CONUNDRUM

THIS FIRST CHAPTER SETS about unpacking the background to a contemporary conundrum that perplexes many people in our pluralistic society. I refer to the realization that while Christians perceive themselves to have been on the back foot, pushed increasingly toward the margins of the public forum for the last one and a half centuries, the typical secular humanist feels the same way. They feel that it is the Christians who have dominated and they who have been disadvantaged. From the perspective of this book, this is a paradox with unfortunate implications for both groups of people. It makes the Christians defensive, feeling that somehow they are wrongly discriminated against and in danger of losing their ancient rights. That they need to gather the faithful to prayer, to turn back the clock, to start up specifically Christian legal initiatives, schools, parties, and lobby groups and generally become increasingly strident in their demands to be heard. The secularists, on the other hand, feel as a result that the Christians are still so very much alive and dominant that they need to make their own position more distinct and to defend in turn those hard-won cultural freedoms and changes in the law that represent their seemingly secular approach to life. The problem is that neither position expresses either the actual strengths or the real weaknesses of the two perspectives and their potential contributions to contemporary society. Both of them, I suggest, are manifesting different aspects of something seriously wrong with the way our society has developed over history and that is coming to a head at this critical time in the Western world.

In order to get our heads around this conundrum and the problem that lies behind it, this chapter traces and explains four stages in the past history of the West. These are: the initial context of Christian faith and political power, the subsumption of transcendence by sovereignty, the circumstances and effects of the fall of the church, and the subsequent era of modernity, postmodernity, and the rejection of transcendence. The sections will work hard to clarify unfamiliar words and subjects, so it will be well worth persevering even if the language appears daunting at first!

(B) FOUR STAGES IN THE DEVELOPMENT OF THE CONTEMPORARY PUZZLE

(1) Christian faith and political power

To understand this conundrum properly, we need to go back a long way, to the very beginning of the relationship between Christian faith and political power. This takes us to the dawn of the Christian era, to around 15 CE, or what used to be called AD 15. This change in the way we record the past centuries is a good place to start, even before we look at what was happening at the time. For it marks a recent shift in understanding Christian history from an assumed common faith where past years are described as "the year of our Lord" (AD: from the Latin *anno domini*), to a multi-faith and no-faith situation where we recognize a past Common Era (CE) from which the contemporary Western world takes its bearings. This change would be put down by many to secularization, or the move from a Christian worldview to one where the Christian faith is mainly only a memory, and the majority perspective is without conscious recourse to Christian religious practice or belief. In this way secularization presents an example of the very puzzle under investigation here, where the Christian feels marginalized but the secular world still feels the lingering impact of what Nietzsche called the shadow[1] of the Christian past.

From the standpoint of this book, the old way of describing past years as "years of our Lord" exposes the heart of the misunderstanding that determined the fall of the church and is the root cause of our conundrum. The muddle revolves around the question of what lordship really means. The year 15 CE locates the point where the answer to this question came into a sharp focus that set the direction for the political system of the Western world to the present day. For it was then that the hierarchical power of empire invaded divinity, that what became known as the cult of Caesar was initiated by Tiberias Caesar when he elevated his father to the status of god at his death. Lordship and transcendence were united as one. This deification of political leadership was not entirely new. It had already emerged in the east of the empire where the practice had been engaged in by past Egyptian empires,

1. Nietzsche, *The Gay Science*, para. 108.

and briefly by the Greek Empire under Alexander the Great. But now it took place at the power center of the most extensive empire that the world had ever seen.

By this time the Roman Empire had existed for over two hundred years and the city of Rome itself for more than seven hundred. While the city and its empire had started out as a republic ruled by a senate of aristocrats, it had been moving towards a totalitarian monarchy for several generations. The development had been gathering momentum under the leadership of Julius Caesar, and came to a head with the emergence of Octavius Caesar as supreme monarch from 31 BCE onwards. By the time of his death in 15 CE, the monarchy was ready for the crowning event of his deification. As by this time the whole known world was under Roman rule through a system of puppet rulers made up of local propertied aristocracy, the emperor Tiberias Caesar was now affirmed as Son of God in his leadership over them all. This was declared to be the case publicly on numerous buildings and substantiated by the presence of the Roman garrisons that secured the *pax Romana*. It was underlined by the taxes regularly collected to pay for it. It is now generally agreed that by the time of Jesus Roman imperial rule was integrated in this way in Israel too, as in other similarly occupied lands, and that the high-priestly family of Annas and Caiaphas who feature in the gospel accounts were Rome's local elite in the south of Israel alongside King Herod in the north.[2]

Given all this, it is striking to realize that in approximately the same year that Tiberias Caesar became Son of God, 15 CE, Jesus was coming of age and questioning the Jewish authorities, according to Luke's narrative.[3] By the time Jesus began his public life, Tiberias Caesar was well established as divine lord with this title commonly displayed

2. Carter, *Matthew and Empire*, 13; Horsley, *Jesus and Empire*, 34.
3. Luke 2:42–47.

in public places.[4] It was into this political arena that Jesus stepped, entering the synagogues and streets with a very different declaration of the government of God, and with himself as the example of a divine lordship in complete contrast to the lordship of Caesar. The gospels' own introduction of Jesus as Son of God,[5] the stories of Satan and the demons' recognition of him as such,[6] and the public questions and taunts about whether he was the Son of God or not,[7] were all in the context of the use of the title to identify the lordship of Caesar. Once this political context is properly understood, then Jesus' frequent emphasis on the true nature of lordship assumes unavoidable significance. Warnings such as "Not everyone who says to Me, 'Lord, Lord,' will enter the kingdom of heaven, but he who does the will of My Father who is in heaven,"[8] take on a whole new political dimension. Debates over "who's the greatest in the kingdom of heaven?"[9] must similarly be understood to question the legitimacy of the Roman order. Jesus' statement "Whoever then humbles himself as this child, he is the greatest in the kingdom of heaven"[10] can be seen to challenge head-on the current assumptions about the nature of both lordship and deity. The radical implications of his intention are even clearer in the discussions at the last supper, when he said, "You know that those who are recognized as rulers of the Gentiles lord it over them; and their great men exercise authority over them. But it is not this way among you . . ."[11] There simply were no other

4. Crossan and Reed, *In Search of Paul*, 74–104.

5. Mark 1:1.

6. Matt 4:6; 8:29.

7. Matt 26:63; 27:40.

8. Matt 7:21.

9. Matt 18:1.

10. Matt 18:4.

11. Mark 10:42–43.

possible existing referents for "the lords of the Gentiles" than the lords of the Romans.

Finally, when John's gospel tells the story of Jesus' vivid depiction of the fullness of transcendence in the incident where Jesus washes his disciples' feet, including Judas's, the counterpolitical nature of lordship in the government of God is clear. It appears that this is what Jesus came to reveal at the critical moment in world history. As he puts it, "You call Me Teacher and Lord; and you are right, for so I am. If I then, the Lord and the Teacher, washed your feet, you also ought to wash one another's feet. For I gave you an example that you also should do as I did to you."[12] This helps give clarity to the nature of the apostle Paul's understanding of the fullness of time.[13] It is the meeting point of times, the moment where the trajectories of God's governance and fallen lordship meet.

From this perspective we can conclude, as contemporary historical and archeological research makes clear, that Jesus' message and demeanor were subversively political from the start. The whole direction of his teaching and practice positions the testimony of Jesus in confrontation with empire and makes the gospel the good news that God's politics is not a dominating transcendence colonized by sovereignty but rather the gift of self-emptying love or *kenosis*.[14] This word "kenosis" is derived from the Greek word *keno* used by the apostle Paul in Philippians chapter 2, and refers to the emptying out of hierarchical power by Jesus, demonstrated throughout the gospel narratives, expressed by the motif of taking up the cross, culminating in Jesus' crucifixion and vindicated by his resurrection. This reversal

12. John 13:13–15.

13. Gal 4:4.

14. As described by the apostle Paul in his famous hymn in Phil 2:5–11.

of imperial sovereignty manifest in the gospel accounts of Jesus' life forms the heart of the kingdom or governance of God. In order to distinguish clearly between sovereignty and the totally different kind of power of God's governance, I use the newly-made-up word *kenarchy*. It is formed out of the Greek words *keno* (to empty) and *arche* (power) and signifies the emptying out of power on behalf of others in contrast with exercising power over others. The full political implications of kenarchy are the subject of the imminent companion volume to this book: *Discovering Kenarchy*. What is clear is that the story of Jesus presents an entirely opposite view of the relationship between God and political power to that demonstrated by the politics of empire.

All that we have considered so far may seem to deepen our conundrum rather than explain it. For not only do we have the question of why two oppositely positioned groups are feeling the same way as each other, we now have the question of why the Christians manifest an attitude which aligns them with the dominating sovereignty of the Romans and not the loving kenosis of Jesus. For that matter, how is it that the secularists who oppose the Christians' perceived attitude do so in the same spirit as the dominating Christians? The next section sheds more light on this.

(2) The subsumption of transcendence by sovereignty

The consequences of the coming together of hierarchical power and divinity in the time of the Roman Empire, where the power exercised by Rome subsumed, or colonized, the generally recognized expression of divinity, extended long after the lifetime of the public cult of the Caesars and became the accepted understanding of lordship throughout Western history. It was this kind of rulership that came to define the combination of church and empire in Europe, known as Christendom, that endured from the beginning of the Middle Ages until the end of the modern era. This again raises the question of how Christians came to adopt the subsumed transcendence that Jesus came so deliberately to expose and challenge. What happened to the testimony of Jesus? How come the church, as Ellen Meiksins Wood has put it, was "transformed from a radical Jewish sect which opposed the temporal authority of Empire, into a doctrine amenable to, and even encouraging, imperial obedience?"[15] Although the deification of the emperor had the effect of powerfully legitimating the dominant expression of political power, it is clear that as far as the first few centuries went, the church managed to maintain its counterpolitical distinctiveness. We have seen how from the beginning the gospel had challenged the puppet leaders of empire within Israel and, as the narratives record, this ultimately led to Jesus' crucifixion by the Roman authorities. In the early years of what has become known as the church, Jesus' followers generally remained true to their counterpolitical stance. As the Book of Acts describes, Peter and John challenged the Jewish authorities with the question, "Whether it is right in the sight of God to give heed to you rather than to God, you be the judge; for we cannot stop speaking about what we have seen and heard."[16] Paul had the same approach to the Jewish council, challenging their dominating approach and insisting on pursuing the confrontation between the two understandings of lordship all the way to Rome itself.[17]

The earliest Christian writings after the New Testament, such as the late-second-century *Epistle to Diognetus*, clearly emphasize the difference between the nature of the

15. Meiksins Wood, *Empire of Capital*, 35.

16. Acts 4:19–20.

17. Acts 23:1–5; 25:10–12.

authority of God and hierarchical lordship. The writer describes God as the One who sent "the very artificer and creator of the universe himself . . . not as a man might suppose, in sovereignty (*tyrannis*) and fear and terror . . . but in gentleness and meekness . . . not compelling, for compulsion is not an attribute of God."[18] Lactantius emphasizes that there are no hierarchical categories in the creator's intention for human relationships. "With him there is no slave or master. Since we all have the same father, so we are all alike his freeborn children. No one is poor in his eyes, except for want of justice; no one is rich, except in moral qualities." He goes on to make a direct contrast between divine and imperial power and asserts: "neither the Romans nor the Greeks could sustain justice, since they had so many levels of disparity in their societies, separating . . . powerless from powerful."[19] But the clear distinction between God's power and the power of empire was a difficult line to hold, as the debates between the disciples and Jesus over the nature of authority within the gospel story make clear. Before long the leaders of the early church began to see themselves as having the same kind of authority as the Roman lords of the Gentiles, despite Jesus' warnings. And the very nature of the transcendence the church was supposed to represent began to look and sound exactly like the characteristics of imperial sovereignty. Seemingly before the end of the first century, bishops took to wearing a ruler's hat like the high priest as a mark of their hierarchical authority. Eusebius of Caesarea quotes Polycrates, the leading bishop in Asia, to the effect that the apostle John adopted this practice.[20] Whether this detail is true or not, the shift within the church towards the same kind of lordship as the Roman political leadership

18. Lake, *The Epistle to Diognetus*, 365.

19. O'Donovan and O'Donovan, *From Irenaeus to Grotius*, 52.

20. Eusebius of Caesarea, *The History of the Church*, 173.

contributed to the bishops' growing tendency to be seen as a threat to the Empire's authority.

In the course of the early centuries of Christian history the power of subsumed transcendence gradually challenged and permeated the radical understanding of authority among Jesus' followers. This can appropriately be described as the original secularization of the church. As a result the political shape of church and empire became more and more alike, until in the fourth century a partnership of the hierarchically organized leaders of the church and the hierarchical authorities of empire marked the fall of the church from the radical testimony of the gospel account and entrenched sovereign power as the accepted means to peace for nearly two millennia. The way to peace was by the exercise of hierarchical power. Sovereignty was the order of the day. At this stage a hidden property of our conundrum was already forming. Our two conflicting groups share this partnership of desire for sovereign power. At the beginning this was a mutually supportive and more or less peaceful partnership. As the next section indicates, in the course of time, the twin foci of power became more competitive and conflictual in the manner seen in our conundrum. But the underlying substance of the partnership was agreed. However, before moving to the way this developed on into the modern world, it is important to explain why I am deliberately choosing the phrase "transcendence subsumed by sovereignty" to describe what took place, so that we can grasp the full significance of what happened.

To subsume means to include something in a larger category or class of things. So to subsume transcendence with sovereignty means to make God part of the category of rulership by hierarchy. But because God is regarded as the highest power, the effect is to make the hierarchical domination that drives empire the supreme power over all.

Empire did not merely associate or cooperate with the divine, it swallowed it up. From now on deity and empire were inextricably connected. The politics of empire determined the lordship of God and the lordship of God affirmed the politics of empire. I have chosen to use the word "transcendence" to describe what was happening, rather than the word "God," because the word "God" has now become so colonized by the mindset of hierarchical power that it tends to connote it subconsciously for us all. This is true of the word "transcendence" too, as we shall see later, but it is sufficiently unfamiliar to some of us that it is slightly more neutral and functions better to make the point that it has a wider potential meaning than a hierarchical God figure. This joining together of hierarchical power and the theology of God has determined the way that the West has understood lordship ever since. Hierarchical power or, to use the more familiar word, sovereignty has characterized the understanding of what it means to be God from that time until today, and still does so today. The argument of this book is that the gospel of Jesus emerged at a precise fullness of times to challenge and overturn this coming together of sovereignty and transcendence. It affirms that the task of Jesus' followers still is and always has been to live out this calling. The fact that, instead of doing so, they embraced the subsumption of transcendence by sovereignty themselves from the fourth century onwards, constitutes the fall of the church. The nature and effect of the fall has been so total that, far from being the antidote to empire, the church has become its primary carrier. As a result the subsumption of transcendence by sovereignty has been made so complete that even when, as we shall see, transcendence was rejected to get rid of the oppression that had become associated with it, the deeply entrenched mindset that the marriage of sovereignty and transcendence had established, remained.

Secular thinking and practice continued to assume that sovereign power was the means to peace.

(3) The circumstances and effects of the fall of the church

The apparent triumph of the subsumption of transcendence by sovereignty and its embrace by the church in the fourth century was rooted in the mistaken belief that it was the same kind of power that God exercised. The first person to fully develop this thinking was Eusebius, who became the bishop of Caesarea in around 314 CE. A friend, supporter, and biographer of the Roman emperor Constantine, he regarded Constantine's conversion, and his introduction of Christianity as the official religion of the Roman Empire, as the evidence of the success of the church and the beginning of the coming kingdom of peace promised by the gospel testimony. Eusebius was a prolific theologian and historian whose writings became enormously influential in the development of the church. He wrote the first-ever known *History of Christianity*, which is still a main source for our knowledge of the early Christian period after the end of the New Testament records. The next chapter will look more closely at the way Eusebius's work choreographed the fall of the church. Suffice it to say at this stage that he developed a version of soteriology that effectively recast the gospel.

The theological word "soteriology" being used here refers to the story of salvation. It interprets what the gospels reveal about the nature of the human condition and what Jesus did to resolve it. Eusebius no longer saw the story as the outpouring of divine love to free the multitude from the oppression of empire by soaking up all the toxic effects of individual and corporate domination, which is the recurrent theme of the gospel account of the life, death, and

resurrection of Jesus. Instead he depicted it in the now familiar terms of God's offended sovereignty and its appeasement
and reconciliation. It is not difficult to see how this justified
the subsumption of transcendence by sovereignty. Hierarchical power was rendered absolute. The human condition was
presented as the consequence of the failure to submit to God's
superior power. Eusebius and those who agreed with him
were seemingly unaware that this rendered God moral only
by virtue of the extent of his power to dominate, and that this
made God immoral even on his own terms. If insisting on
our own way and power is sin, then why is it not sin for God
to insist on his own way and power? Is it only because his
power is greater than ours? But if so, he is worse than us, not
better. Repentance for failure to obey this dominating God
restored the culprit to favor by means of the appeasement of
his wrath by the substitution of the sacrifice of Jesus in place
of the punishment otherwise meted out to those who refused
to submit. Then, from the position of restored relationship
to God's authority over the creation and the rest of humanity
within it, the fallen sinner could now operate properly within
the hierarchical order of church and empire.

It is a mark of the penetration of this mindset that
many people do a double take when they hear the story of
salvation set out like this. At first they cannot hear anything
strange about it. Or if they can, to criticize it seems dishon-
oring or disrespectful to God. However, it is the argument
of this book that such a way of understanding God and the
gospel is far from the testimony of Jesus or the good news
of the gospel. It is this misunderstanding of God that lies
at the heart of the fall of the church and sustains a yoke
of domination held together by both church and state to
the present day. Hence both Christians and secularists feel
dominated and marginalized. The next chapter tells the
story of how intensive theological and historical research

brought me to this conclusion. However, to give a precise overview of the way in which this version of the salvation story has brought about the deep structural misalignment that gives rise to the current conundrum, it may be helpful at this stage to spell out as clearly as possible the basic components of Eusebius's subsumed soteriology.

i.   God is the ultimate hierarchical power that must be submitted to.

ii. The failure to submit incurs retribution, the nature of which is death.

iii. This penalty can be exchanged for the blood spilt in the violent death of Jesus on the cross.

iv. Repentant submission to God's order in church and empire, and the constant reenactment of Jesus' sacrificial death through regular participation in the eucharist, makes a way for the followers of Jesus to experience the coming outworking of God's reign of peace.

In the course of the centuries following this redirection of the meaning of the gospel story, these key components developed in several significant ways, but remained firmly supportive of the supremacy of sovereign power. Firstly, the understanding of God as absolute hierarchical ruler led to a return to the Old Testament law as the basis for theology and politics, despite Jesus' clear teaching, continued by the apostle Paul, that the law was brought to its full end in him. Secondly, the role of violent sacrifice as the means to uphold sovereign power framed the way the eucharist was understood, and justified the violent sacrifice of human life in war and work for the maintenance and defense of peace; this despite Jesus' instruction to love your enemies, give to those who beg from you, and recognize that mercy triumphed over judgment.[21] Thirdly, the idea that God

---

21. Luke 6:27, 30; Matt 9:13.

needed appeasing for our failure to submit to his superior power led to the idea of paying for peace and liberty, despite the implications of the gospel that peace on earth was God's free gift to be received by faith. Together these mutually reinforcing theological and political developments justified the power of sovereignty as it continued to dominate the history of the West.

(4) Modernity, postmodernity, and the rejection of transcendence

By the twelfth century, the partnership of the church with the expressions of empire that developed after the fall of Rome had become increasingly marked by the curtailment of human freedom and creativity. The period of extraordinary artistic, scientific, and intellectual creativity that is known in its formative phase as the Renaissance, and that culminated by the seventeenth century in what is called the Enlightenment, attempted to throw off this yoke. The very word "Enlightenment" connotes the sense of darkness and ignorance with which transcendence was increasingly associated and the newfound emphasis on human reason that attempted to break through it. This was a time when the struggle for freedom of expression reached the point at which intellectual thought opposed reason against revelation and ecclesiastical authority but failed to see that the problem was not necessarily transcendence but sovereignty itself. As a result the modern era that followed was blind to its own dependence on sovereignty to achieve human freedom, and both the church and the secular world continued to embody and compete in imperial power.

It is this confusion over sovereignty that continued to shape what has become our contemporary paradox and led to the adversarial positioning of the church and the secular world. For despite the deep agreement over the necessity of sovereignty as the means to peace, the new humanists of modernity saw the religious legitimation of sovereignty as the source of the oppression, rather than the operation of sovereignty itself. Suspicion and rejection of the church and its doctrines increasingly came to characterize the modern age. The use of the term "modern" or "modernity" here is a technical one which refers to the whole period from the Enlightenment until the mid twentieth century. The period after the world wars until the present day is generally referred to as "postmodernity" and is marked by the turn away from dependence on rationality and science towards a new skepticism about foundational certainties and a preference for open-ended narratives as a means of talking about life and the universe.

The story of my research, which forms the content of the next chapter, has convinced me that this whole period of Western history continued to be driven by the underlying assumption that the ownership and exercise of sovereign power was the means to peace and prosperity. This was particularly true of those well-known happenings such as the Reformation, the emergence of the nation state, the revolutions in France, America, and Russia, and the European wars of empire culminating in the First and Second World Wars. The fact that the shift from absolute power to multiplied sovereignty after the genocidal carnage of the Thirty Years War in the mid seventeenth century was eventually succeeded three centuries later by a twentieth century of similar carnage, demonstrates just how deeply the peace through sovereignty mindset ran. So even when the bold, confident, disciplinary sovereignty of modernity was partly crushed by the human cost of war, the ugliness of the Russian communist experiment, and the nuclear proliferation of the Cold War, it was still the surviving memory of the transcendent culture of Christianity that bore the brunt of the blame. Instead of the focus of attention being, at last, the foundations of the domination system itself, and the stages of its transition through history to the present day, such as this book is endeavoring to set out, critics in the transition to postmodernity that followed remained fixed in the fight against transcendence. Serious postmodern thinkers such as Michel Foucault[22] and neo-Marxists like Michael Hardt and Antonio Negri[23] who helpfully explain the defining factor of contemporary political power as the commodification of life itself, or *biopower*, continue to insist on a complete break between the past and present cultural worlds of modernity and postmodernity. We will consider the characteristics of biopower shortly.

The simple narrative of the subsumption, or colonization, of transcendence by sovereignty that I am putting forward here, strikes at the heart of all the favored shibboleths surrounding the four defining events of modern Western history referred to above. It also challenges what I perceive to be the fifth, newly emerging one. To begin with it sets aside the view that the Protestant Reformation brought about a fundamental reform of the Western church and society. While recognizing that the Reformation introduced many to a direct experience of God and made significant inroads into the absolute politics of the sovereign hierarchies of church and empire, this soon transitioned into new forms of hierarchical power represented by the sovereignty of the People, the nation state, and the new capitalism that undergirded it. Secondly, instead of viewing the nation state and its supposed separation of church and state as a positive development, it sees the nation state as the dependent child of the partnership of church and empire. From this

22. Foucault, *The History of Sexuality,* vol. I.
23. Hardt and Negri, *Empire; Multitude.*

perspective the assumption that the Western democratic nation state upholds the separation of politics and religion is an unjustifiable deception. Thirdly, rather than regarding the Second World War as a defining fight between an evil fascist empire and a now free West, it contends that the difference between Nazi Germany and the previous empires of Europe was only one of degree. It asserts that its mistake was to attempt the same kind of colonial superiority in the homelands of Europe that the previous European empires had exercised in the more distant continents of Africa, Australasia, and America. Fascism and so-called liberal representative democracy are on the same political spectrum as each other. Fourthly, it makes the same point about communism and capitalism and suggests that the only fundamental difference between communism and capitalism is that one relies on a socialist form of sovereign power whereas the other relies on a capitalist form. Hence it is to be expected that the collapse of communism in the East, far from vindicating the superiority of the capitalist system of the West, prefigures its inability to deliver the still-expected peace and its own rapid and inevitable decomposition.

Finally it challenges the postmodern insistence that a total break has occurred between the modern world of certainty and moral absolutes and the postmodern world of relativism and pluralism. Based on their opinion that the former disciplinary society was dependent on an enduring transcendence for its operation, Foucault and others with him tried to protect postmodernity from any resurgence of the oppression of Christendom while retaining some hope for a coming peace. Actually the insight and the hope of prophetic thinkers like Foucault and the neo-Marxists could be strengthened by the recognition that biopower is simply part of the genealogy of church and sovereignty. Once we recognize that the subsumed version of the salvation story has consolidated the idea that sovereignty must be bought at the cost of violent victimhood for there to be peace, then it is not hard to see how the nation state ends up devouring itself and its people in order to sustain its sovereignty. As Foucault explains, human life, or biopower, has become the raw material of the machine that drives the Western political system.

From this standpoint it is possible to see that our contemporary conundrum is more than the result of losing Jesus' loving kenotic lordship, forming a consequential conflictual partnership in sovereignty, and then blaming each other for the destructive fall out. It also presents contemporary evidence of the final destination of the pursuit of sovereignty. Instead of a place of peace, sovereignty reduces humanity to the fodder of the Western capitalist system. Here, the only real value of human life is to supply the circular routine of feeding the sovereignty that oppresses it, and in order to preserve the domination system, I become its victim. The marginalization and powerlessness felt by Christians and secularists alike is coming neither from transcendence nor the fear of it but from the age-old belief that human beings need sovereign power to fulfill their present and future hope for peace. It is a false hope consolidated in the subsumption of transcendence by sovereignty, its embrace by the church, the West's subsequent narrative of domination, and its various attempts to escape its oppression until its final descent into biopower. It is the message of this book that the real hope for future peace is neither a partnership in sovereignty nor the misguided attempt to separate sovereignty from transcendence but the rediscovery of a transcendence free from sovereign power.

2

The Story Unfolds

(A) THE CENTRALITY OF SOVEREIGNTY

I FIRST ENGAGED WITH the idea of the fall of the church as
a result of trying to answer pressing questions about life
in the contemporary West. The conundrum investigated
in the first chapter is one significant example. Other related questions include the following: why has the assumption of progress towards peace and prosperity persisted
throughout Western history despite the prevalence of war
and poverty? Given Western democratic institutions, why
do the politics of power and the commodification of human worth increasingly characterize society? And how is it
that even the best of church experience in both traditional
and radical expressions so often tends to relapse into hierarchical domination and control? It seemed to me that
these questions could best be understood and answered if
there had been a point at which the church and its theology colluded with the politics of violence and domination

and displaced the testimony of Jesus. I started my research by focusing on the present and then headed back nearly two millennia in search of explanations for my contemporary questions. As the career of Eusebius of Caesarea and the reign of Constantine represent the point at which Christianity and empire officially came together, it was an obvious place to start.

This chapter highlights the factors which, in line with Eusebius's core soteriology outlined in chapter 1, indicate a collusion so serious that it can appropriately be described as the fall of the church. It shows how this came about through the mistaken assumption that real hope for peace is dependent on the proper exercise of the politics of sovereignty. It then traces the way that this error was turned into theology by Eusebius and his successors and became a dominant legitimating myth of Western society. The chapter concentrates on the key elements of Eusebius's counterfeit story of salvation, tracing them in their present-day versions and back through history. These can be summed up as three interrelated operations of government: sovereign power, sovereign law, and sovereign payment. As the role of appeasement and payment is so central to his narrative of the salvation story, I refer to all three of these together as the "currency" of Western civilization. It is the conclusion of my research that in the course of history they culminated in the debt-based system of promissory notes and computer digits we now call money and which today consumes the raw material of life itself. This chapter begins to explore the story of that development.

But first it is time to take a closer look at the use of the words "peace," "power," and "sovereignty" in this context and in the book so far. I am using the word "peace" here in accord with its Hebrew roots in two ways. Firstly, it is used to carry the broad sense of the Hebrew word for peace, *shalom*, as wholeness, health, and fullness across the whole experience of life in creation, in contrast with the narrower sense of merely peace of mind or absence of conflict. Secondly, I am affirming its strong connection with the Hebrew prophetic stream, where the prospect of *shalom* is used as a futuristic hope from which to criticize the seemingly insurmountable injustices of the political status quo.[1] As historians such as N. T. Wright have made clear, it was this Hebrew prophetic stream that formed the back-story to the message of Jesus and his kingdom.[2] It was the idea that this kind of peace came not through the power of love but through sovereign power that led to the corruption of the gospel testimony.

I take the word "power" to refer to the means by which an individual or group attempts to achieve their will in the context of the world situation in which they find themselves. By this definition the word "sovereignty" is a power word, for it describes a particular means whereby an individual or group rule over the rest. However, whereas "power" is a neutral word and does not determine the particular way in which desire is pursued and carried out, this is not the case with sovereignty. The standard dictionary definition of the word "sovereign" is "a supreme ruler, especially a monarch."[3] The same entry goes on to describe "sovereignty" as "suzerainty, hegemony, dominion, rule, reign, pre-eminence, power, jurisdiction, authority, leadership, command, sway, supremacy, ascendancy, primacy; kingship, queenship." The meaning of the first word on the list, "suzerainty," is given later under "suzerain" as "a feudal

---

1. See, for example, Isa 9:6–7; 32; 55:12; Ezek 34:25; Zech 8:12.

2. See Mitchell, *Church, Gospel, & Empire*, 211.

3. See, for example, *The Reader's Digest Oxford Complete Word Finder*, 1484.

overlord."[4] Some of the definitions listed above, like power, could be used to refer to a neutral exercise of leadership authority. But the association of sovereign and sovereignty with words such as "hegemony" and "pre-eminence," which unequivocally describe hierarchical status and behavior, makes them a carrier of imperial politics and this is the way I am using them here. It is the conclusion of my research that, even if the words "sovereign" and "sovereignty" could be used neutrally, the subsumption of transcendence by sovereignty and the subsequent partnership of church and empire have ruined them for any further use in this way. So, to summarize, the word "power" in this book is a neutral one, and is also used to refer to the power of love and kenosis, whereas the words "sovereign" and "sovereignty" refer to a hierarchical, unequal system of rule where leaders assume power over others, whether apparently for their good, or deliberately in order to oppress them. Both ends of the scale, sovereignty for good or sovereignty for deliberate oppression, are regarded as a continuum of domination and alien to the peace of humanity and the lordship of Jesus.

(B) THE DEVELOPING COMPONENTS OF THE WESTERN SYSTEM

The three components of sovereignty embedded in Eusebius's soteriology, sovereign power, sovereign law, and sovereign payment, coincide with the basic constructs of empire. The Roman Empire was essentially a form of political rule in which sovereignty was imposed by threat or acts of violence, consolidated by the institution of law, and paid for by a combination of tax and patrony where clients paid respect to victorious military generals or former aristocratic slave

4. Ibid., 1574.

owners in return for their "freedom." The first of the four sections which follow focuses on the connection between this equation and Eusebius's interpretation of the salvation story. The second emphasizes its ongoing function as what I have come to regard as the central underlying myth of the contemporary West. The third and fourth sections drill down at two significant intervening points in history. While it is to be expected that if this thesis is accurate, some of the same kinds of discoveries would be found wherever we might dig, the chosen locations help uncover some of the key developments that help make sense of our contemporary situation.

(1) Salvation and empire

(a) The necessity of monarchy

Eusebius believed that monarchical order was rooted in God's nature and was an essential moral quality of all leadership. Extensive research makes clear that this moral understanding of sovereignty was central to his construction of the salvation story, and fully manifest in his understanding of the authority of God and that of the bishops and emperor who represented him. Many assessments of Eusebius's work dismiss him prematurely as simply what is known as a panegyrist or eulogist. These were names given to a writer, often officially appointed, whose job it was to convey a flattering perspective on the life and achievements of a famous leader, either on the occasion of an important anniversary or as an obituary. From this perspective, the language Eusebius uses to align the monarchy[5] of God, the

5. The word "monotheism" was only introduced in the seventeenth century; before then monarchy was used of both God and earthly rulers.

Emperor Constantine, and the bishop of Tyre might seem deliberately exaggerated. However, the work of M. J. Hollerich on Eusebius's little-known commentary on Isaiah sheds new light on all this.[6] It makes clear that far from taking a culturally determined, superficial approach, Eusebius was a serious theologian whose opinions were deeply rooted in his understanding of the essential part played by sovereignty in bringing about the eschatological, or final, peace that was basic to the outcome of the salvation story.

Eusebius's serious theological work affirms the points he makes in his more popular books, *The Life of Constantine*, *An Oration in Praise of Constantine*, and *The History of the Church*. For Eusebius, the monarchical sovereignty of God was the very axis of the world order.[7] He was convinced that pluralism, either in politics or deity, was the enemy of peace. In his understanding of the natural and spiritual worlds, pluralism was demonic; any other god than the Christian God was a demon, and any plurality in political leadership was sustained by these demons.[8] In his view it was the activity of Jesus on the cross that had paved the way for the fullness of church and empire that was manifesting in Constantine's Rome.[9] Jesus' appeasement of God's offended sovereignty had overcome the demons of pluralism and paved the way for the now-emerging sovereign peace.

(b) The role of law and creed

In his *Commentary on Isaiah*, Eusebius develops the concept of what he calls "godly polity," by which he means a

---

6. Hollerich, *Eusebius of Caesarea's Commentary on Isaiah*.

7. See Mitchell, *Church, Gospel, & Empire*, 34.

8. Ibid., 37, 39.

9. Ibid., 36, 37.

hierarchical order of society administered by monarchical bishops over cities and regions.[10] With the political and liturgical demise of Israel as the identifiable people of God, the church is presented by Eusebius as the inheritor of the priestly theocratic community. But this theocracy, or rule by God, is not now in the context of a specific land but in relation to the empire's universal peace. The evidence and outcome of this peace was, for Eusebius, to be seen in the orderly submission of the people to the emperor's laws and the church to its councils.

Viewed in this light, contemporary research puts a whole different slant on the purpose and outcome of the church councils from that which has been generally supposed. The Council of Nicaea that Constantine called and presided over, and the creeds which he helped draw up there, eventually became the basis for the universal sovereignty of pope and emperor. Rather than primarily being about theological truth, their purpose was subordinated to the unity of thought and clarity of content necessary to the exercise of sovereign power. This does not mean that Eusebius and Constantine were intentionally deceptive or manipulative. They simply assumed that the exercise of sovereign power was central to the divine nature and therefore its image in the behavior of human beings. Research shows that the controversies about the relationship between the universally Sovereign God and his Son, which formed a main focus of the Council and Creed of Nicaea and subsequent councils and formulations, were intimately connected to the related matter being literally fought out between Constantine and his rival Licinius at exactly the same time.[11] The question of whether there was a single primary power vested in divine lordship was less a theo-

10. Ibid., 31.
11. Ibid., 48, 49.

retical matter and more the practical temporal question of whether an empire could have more than one Caesar. The unity of the church and the supremacy of the one God were seen to be essential to the function of the emperor and his *pax Romana*.

(c) The centrality of appeasement

It is likely that the use of priestly sacrifices to appease the gods, already established in the polytheism of Greek and Rome, had helped normalize paying for the privilege of the Roman imperial peace in the mind of the multitude. However, once the idea of one God as ultimate sovereign was joined to the concept of an ultimate appeasement to match the offence of disobeying him, the practice of paying the authorities for a peace brought about by the exercise of hierarchical power was legitimated much more strongly. The church's proclamation of this gospel, its affirmation via the hierarchical positions and legal determinations of the church and state, and its continual reenactment in the mass were seen as fundamental to the coming peace of the kingdom of God. It is my argument that this conjunction of an absolutely sovereign God whose laws must be obeyed, with an ultimate appeasement to insure the peaceful operation of his sovereign rule, has sustained the mindset of empire in its various forms from Constantine's Rome until its so-called "secular" expression in the present day.

I am not suggesting that the idea of exchange or payment for things is bad in or of itself. There is nothing essentially wrong with trade, exchange, or the use of money. Jesus taught about the loving application of these activities, in making friends and caring for the victims of crime, for example.[12] The problem that I am focusing on is the one

12. Luke 10:30–37; 16:1–11.

brought about by the positive association of exchange and payment with appeasement, and its universal application through making this connection central to our understanding of salvation and the cross. It is because the cross and resurrection are so central to the incarnation as the consummation of the gift of love that its association with a payment that brings about an appeasement is so detrimental. It makes appeasement by payment basic to the nature of the relationship between God and humanity, and between humans and each other. Instead of love and gift being established as the key motivations of human life and peace, payment and exchange take their place. The broad pathway to salvation through capitalism, commodification, and ultimately biopower was opened up by this cosmic connection, and the rest, as they say, is history.

(2) The hidden gospel of the West

This mistaken and corrupted interpretation of the central element of the Christian gospel still remains deeply imbedded in the Western mindset. To recognize it exposes the peculiar problematics of the questions outlined at the beginning of the chapter. If the only way to bring about peace and prosperity is by the operation of sovereign power appeased by money and enforced by war, it is hardly surprising that war and poverty have persisted throughout Western history. Similarly, if the foundation of Western democratic institutions is sustained by the idea of peace through sovereign power, and that power has to be bought, then it is likely that the politics of power and the commodification of human worth will come to characterize such a society, despite the eventuality of universal suffrage. And if it is true that the basis of God's own character and his dealings with the human race consists in the exercise of hierarchical sovereignty by law and appeasement, is it strange that the best of church experience in both traditional and radical expressions transpires to be all about hierarchical domination, correct doctrine, and the control of finance?

Put like this, it is obvious that something has gone very wrong. The stark conclusion has to be that the idea of peace through sovereign power is not the testimony of Jesus. The argument of this book and the research behind it is that a "wrong" myth has obscured and displaced the true myth of Jesus portrayed in the gospel accounts, and that this misconceived construct continues to legitimate the contemporary West at the deepest level. Any overview of the immediate operations of politics today typically reveals the components of the currency of sovereignty. This happens to be the week that the revelations of the extent of child abuse perpetrated by the late BBC entertainment personality Jimmy Savile is dominating the news. In response to the BBC's own *Panorama* exposé, Krish Kandiah of the UK Evangelical Alliance remarked on his personal twitter account: "shocking listening to the Jimmy Savile story on Panorama-why is it so hard to question authority?"[13] To which I replied, "Our whole Western mindset assumes hierarchical authority is the way to peace and we Christians carry huge responsibility for it." While the BBC carries a not undeserved reputation as an example of responsible freedom in broadcasting at a superficial level, as a public institution it affirms the deep structures that we are looking at here. This week, as I write, is the beginning of the Remembrance Day period here in the UK, an annual event commemorating the sacrifice of millions of soldiers in the promotion and defense of the Western nation state during and since the First World War. The general willingness to honor the Western military casualties of the current so-called "War

13. https://twitter.com/krishk.

on Terror" and their addition to the national memorials to the fallen soldiers of the twentieth-century European wars of empire reveals how ongoing the myth still is. The often-brave victims are honored for their payment of the ultimate price because this is still the accepted way to peace. Virtually every BBC television announcer, and the vast majority of public or private individuals that appear on television over these three weeks, will wear a prominent red poppy. The same is also the case for the so-called independent channels. The war memorials and annual civic ceremonies of remembrance in the villages, towns, and cities of Britain, its Western allies, and their ex-colonial equivalents continue to promulgate the myth at the state altars. On Remembrance Day itself in Britain, the Queen and senior members of the royal family, the leaders of the Anglican church, of which the Queen is the supreme governor, together with leaders of the other main British faith communities annually affirm the indebtedness of the British nation state to the sacrifice of its youth in war in a solemn ritual at the Cenotaph in Whitehall. They are joined by the leaders of the armed forces, the Prime Minister and senior leaders of the government, the leaders of the opposition, the commonwealth ambassadors, and leaders of business and industry. There is no better explanation for the ease with which the multitude supplies the taxes, cultural support, and human volunteers for battle necessary for the endurance of the Western system than the enduring power of Eusebius's soteriological myth and its ongoing enforcement.

The philosopher Giorgio Agamben provides real insight into the foundational connection between the Western world and the currency of sovereignty. He uses terms that take a bit of grasping but it is worth the effort. Drawing on the ideas of Carl Schmidt, he explains what he calls the state of the exception behind law.[14] By this he refers to the

14. Agamben, *State of Exception*.

potential that any governing power has to suspend the law. So whatever the motive that leads a government to suspend the law, is revealed to be the absolute power behind the law, or that to which the law is subject. It turns out that in the contemporary West, this boils down to the pursuit of sovereign power as an end in itself. Anything that stands in its way, even those things which apparently protect its role in securing peace, must be prevented at all costs. So laws, human rights, social provisions, and economic protections that seemingly uphold justice for the multitude, can be open to suspension if sovereignty is under threat. Agamben uses the example of the suspension of all rights for the prisoners of the War on Terror who were incarcerated in Guantanamo Bay. Barak Obama's inability to close the camp in his first term of office, despite his preelection promises to do so, only serves to underline this.

The response to the current economic crisis provides another similar example. Austerity cuts are being imposed despite the suffering of the poorest. So once again, instead of Jesus' call to bless the poor, comes their neglect in the cause of sovereignty. The nuclear bomb is the ultimate example of the state of exception. It turns out that the final purpose of empire is not peace but either the survival of the most powerful or the destruction of everybody. The neo-Marxist philosophers Michael Hardt and Antonio Negri helpfully show us where this all takes us when they point to the loss of a necessary love motivation for the pursuit of peace for the multitude.[15] Amazingly, they still look to Judeo-Christian love as the remedy for this loss, an insight that is taken up seriously in chapter 4.

15. Hardt and Negri, *Multitude*, 352.

(3) The gospel according to Christendom

Digging back in time to the late Middle Ages, it is possible to trace the persistence and development of Eusebius's salvation myth without much difficulty. We can see how the establishment of sovereign power through war and violent sacrifice, its enshrinement in law, and its legitimation by the appeasement myth were promulgated by theologians such as Pope Innocent III and his predecessor Hildebrand. Emperors like Charlemagne and his eventual successor Frederick II, Pope Innocent's ward and eventual nemesis, drew on the same currency to substantiate their claims to power. Building on the foundations laid by Eusebius and his successors, the essential components of sovereign power were developed in three significant ways.

(a) Securing sovereign power

With the eventual collapse of Rome in the West in 476 CE, a vacuum followed which led to the division and conflict of power between the Eastern and Western churches, popes, and potential emperors, and between them all and the Muslim empire that arose in its wake. As a result, two very important developments took place to justify the various claims to papal and imperial authority and to legitimate its violent promotion and defense. Consequently, instead of an imperial peace there was a bloody fight for the possession of sovereign power. The first of these developments reinterpreted the gospel testimony to such an extent that, in flagrant disregard for the lowly, loving lord, Jesus was recast as an earthly King. This was achieved by emphasizing his lineage as King David's son, not in recognition of the fullness of monarchy and to bring it to an end, but in justification of it. By correlating the anointing of the Spirit directly with the Old Testament anointing of high priest and king, Eusebius's articulation of sovereign power was extended to such a degree that rather than simply displacing the gospel Jesus, he was now reinvented as an earthly monarch. The twelfth-century theologian Norman Anonymous recognized that the circumstances of Jesus' birth and life clearly eschewed all association with temporal monarchical power and its symbols of palace, throne, and riches. As a result, he suggested, quite without awkwardness, that the Roman emperor Tiberias, the agent of the subsumption of transcendence by sovereignty, was to be preferred to Jesus as an example of Christ's earthly kingship.[16]

The second development greatly strengthened the soteriological myth of peace through sovereignty in the interest of protecting the papacy and its lands, and recruiting armies for the defense of the so-called Holy Land. By the end of the twelfth century the violence necessary to reestablish sovereign power was sanctified by what Innocent III termed *negotium crucis* (the business of the cross). Simply put, Innocent argued from Jesus' violent death in support of God's sovereignty that the physical wounds and sacrifices experienced in war were an imitation of, and an actual participation in, the sufferings of Jesus on the cross. In this way the call to arms in the service of empire was termed "taking the cross."[17] What Walter Wink has called the myth of redemptive violence[18] was established at the heart of Western Christendom by making the violent struggle for sovereign power part of discipleship itself.

16. See Mitchell, *Church, Gospel, & Empire*, 83.

17. Ibid., 73–75.

18. Wink, "Facing the Myth of Redemptive Violence."

(b) Constituting sovereign law

In the midst of the threat of loss of sovereign power and
the desire to maintain it, hierarchical leaders of church and
empire like Innocent III and Frederick II relied heavily on
the development of law. In Innocent's case this was canon
law, and in Frederick's case the revival and reenactment of
Roman law. It is not hard to see that, in the volatile situation
of the time, a strong dependence on law was necessary to
defend or establish papal authority or that of one or another
of the competing monarchs as their appropriate partners.
The need to establish the objectivity of law and truth was
greatly strengthened at this point by the quest to reinforce
sovereign power. The justification for the currency of peace
had been the reality of the *pax Romana*. The salvation story
undergirded this. But the imperial peace was now giving
way to war and conflict. To meet this, the legal compo-
nent in Eusebius's soteriology that understood God's law
to be upheld in the atonement by violent retribution was
strengthened so as to encompass canon and state law upheld through war and diplomacy through the business of
the cross. Alongside the recourse to Roman law, a strong
draw was made on ancient Greek rational formulations as
articulated by Aristotle and Plato, which already presumed
the primacy of hierarchical thought forms. This had particular impact on the natural law theories developed by
Thomas Aquinas, which increasingly gave way after the
Renaissance and Reformation to the humanistic rational
and "objective" theories of positivism, Darwinism, and
Evangelical fundamentalism. The important thing to grasp
here is that far from being an objective development of law
for its own sake, this was really the subjection of law to the
cause of sovereign power and helped to constitute the state
of the exception described by Agamben and considered

earlier. I am emphatically not saying here that there is no such thing as truth or objectivity. I am neither claiming that rational thought or scientific endeavor is bad, nor that there is no positive use of law. But when truth and law are formulated and appealed to for the purposes of justifying sovereign power, then they take on a whole new character. This is what the apostle Paul is referring to when he asserts that "the letter kills, but the Spirit gives life."[19] The testimony of Jesus makes clear that the role of truth and law is to be submitted to the kenotic truth of love and relationship. As the gospel of John puts it, "This is eternal life, that they may know You, the only true God, and Jesus Christ whom You have sent."[20] The coming companion volume, *Discovering Kenarchy*, explores this relational basis for knowledge in greater depth.

(c) Transacting sovereign payment

In order to survive, these competing authorities needed resourcing by payments of tithe, tax, or serfdom. We have already noted that the alignment between the subsumption of transcendence by sovereignty and the necessity for the appeasement of offended sovereignty became the means to justify such payments. Such economics of empire, I suggest, both contributed to and were greatly strengthened by a crucial shift in the understanding of the body of Christ that took place sometime in the middle of the twelfth century. As the recent work of Henri de Lubac has made clear, up until then the true body of Christ was generally seen to be the Jesus of the gospel accounts, and the church as the body of disciples living out that same incarnational

19. 2 Cor 3:6.
20. John 17:3.

life in dependence on him.[21] The bread and wine of the eucharist were viewed as the symbolic or mystical body of Christ. However, a shift took place whereby this order was reversed. The gospel testimony to Jesus and the subsequent community of his ecclesia[22] were taken to be the mystical body, and the elements of the communion liturgy became the true body. This had a profound impact that came to a climax in the fourth Lateran Council in 1215 when the doctrine of transubstantiation was inaugurated into canon law, and the mystical symbols were constituted as the actual body of Christ. Hence the enactment of the eucharist became the actual appeasement of God's offended sovereignty. The consequence was that the liturgy of the church and the cultural life of the late Middle Ages came to center around a payment for peace made by the offering of the body of Jesus. The central argument of the Protestant reformers that this only happened once, in an actual historical sacrifice at Calvary, while weakening the role of the papal priesthood who offered this sacrifice on a daily basis, did nothing to reverse this core shift. The Reformation, despite its laudable rejection of indulgences as a means of paying for salvation, failed to reach behind the corruption of the salvation story to the heart of appeasement itself. As a result, the daily exchange taking place in the mass, and thus substantiating payment for sovereignty in the heart of the system, was replaced by an equally mistaken Protestant emphasis on a once-and-for-all payment to God by Jesus on the cross. The myth of peace through payment continued to be endorsed by church theology and practice.

21. de Lubac, *Corpus Mysticum*, 80.

22. The Greek word for "church," used here to distinguish it from the institution that embodied it subsequent to the fourth-century fall.

(4) King Billy and the Bank

There were several reasons why I chose the latter years of the eighteenth century as the second intermediate point in Western history at which to dig down. It was the period of the establishment of what is now known as the modern era. It was the point at which the nation state came into being as the inheritor of the powers of empire and in the interests of which the supposed separation of church and state began its course. At its heart was the founding of the Bank of England. In all, it was the time in which the development of Eusebius's soteriology effectively choreographed the now familiar convolutions of the modern world. It therefore provides an ideal platform on which to examine the unfolding dynamics of the currency of the West. It reveals, in plain view, the way in which the currency of sovereignty literally culminated in the debt-based system of promissory notes, eventually to become computer digits, that we now call money. In order to follow the action more closely, the next three sections trace the development of the three components of this currency, with which we are now becoming familiar.

(a) Multiplying sovereignty

The period of competition and conflict that characterized the attempt to secure the sovereign power of the church and its potential imperial partners following the end of Rome in the West, ultimately culminated in the Thirty Years War. This was a ghastly conflagration that devastated central Europe and in which approximately eight million people lost their lives. It ended with *the Peace of Westphalia*, a series of peace treaties signed between May and October 1648. It is generally recognized that this marked the shift from the old universal sovereign powers to the new nation states of constitutional monarchy or republic. But while it had now become increasingly accepted that sovereignty exercised universally over the whole continent was no longer the way to peace, but rather the route to war and destruction, this by no means brought the currency of sovereign power to an end. Instead it led to the multiplication of sovereignty as the means to peace through the emergence of a plurality of nation states beginning with the Dutch Republic and the constitutional monarchy that emerged in Britain at the end of the seventeenth century. War and diplomacy remained the primary methods for establishing these new nation states, and law and payment continued to be the means of their consolidation. The fact that they still carried the genus of empire and depended on its currency was soon obvious, and it was not long before they manifested their own imperial properties although generally within the accepted framework of multiple sovereignties. Arguably the foremost pioneers of this new expression of sovereign power were William of Orange and the innovative Episcopalian Gilbert Burnet.[23] Through his experience in the Dutch Republic, William had learnt how a limited monarchy could play a crucial role in a developing parliamentary democracy. Burnet's upbringing and early career as a clergyman in Scotland and England had helped him develop a brand of Anglicanism known as latitudinarianism, a word big enough for its sizeable task. This task was to create a church broad enough to encompass a majority of both high and low churchmanship and able to work in tandem with a parliamentary system where the separation of powers allowed both church and state to maintain a degree of sovereignty. Together they transitioned the church and the monarchy into a reconstituted partnership with parliamentary de-

23. See Mitchell, *Church, Gospel, & Empire*, Ch. 4.

mocracy. William III of Orange, who became William III of England, where he reigned alongside his wife Mary, was the infamous King Billy who imposed Protestantism on Ireland. It is easier to understand the ferocity with which he set about this when it is seen in the context of the attempt to overcome the destructive pretensions of the Catholic Church and the French king Louis XIV to monopolize sovereign power.

The overall effect of this transition from universal to multiplied, limited sovereignty was that the payment myth became embodied almost completely in money. The war and diplomacy against universal sovereignty had to be paid for, the increasingly "secular" state had to be financed, and a way had to be found for the rising bourgeoisie to purchase a measure of sovereign power for themselves without impoverishing the already existing sovereign powers. It was to meet this financial need that William Paterson set about persuading parliament to found the Bank of England. But first of all let's take a look at the motivation behind the developing system of parliamentary law that affirmed his plan.

(b) The motivation behind nation states, democratic institutions, and the separation of powers

When William of Orange and Gilbert Burnet disembarked with their army at Torbay in 1688, it was at the invitation of the parliament, who wished to oust the then king, James II. James was a Catholic convert who had inherited the throne on the death of his brother, Charles II, after the restoration of the monarchy subsequent to the English civil war and Cromwell's commonwealth. In the view of William, Burnet, and their parliamentary allies, James's Catholicism made him a natural accomplice of the Pope and the French King Louis XIV, whose pretensions to universal power threatened the independent sovereignty of Britain and the progress of multiplied sovereignty. In advance of their offensive, Burnet had drafted a legal document which had been adopted by parliament, entitled *A Declaration of Reasons for appearing in arms in the Kingdom of England*. It presented William's expedition as "a necessary preservative of English right and freedoms, which all honest and law-abiding subjects must support."[24] It made the unequivocal point that the king could not act legally without the rest of parliament. However, this was really a superficial use of parliamentary law and only an apparent separation of the powers of church and state. That this was the case was soon seen when it gave way to Eusebius's developing soteriological myth. For once William was in place, Burnet, in sermons and speeches to the parliament, drew again on arguments for Christ's earthly kingship to claim that Britain was the inheritor of Israel's theocratic destiny. This transition of peace through universal sovereignty to peace through limited, multiplied sovereignty, vouchsafed by the corrupted gospel story, has continued to reoccur throughout the history of the British Empire and on into the history and self-understanding of the United States of America. The kingdom of God and the partnership in sovereignty of church and empire have continued to be confused with each other.

(c) The money trick

By 1694 the cost of war and diplomacy had tripled what it had cost to exercise sovereign power in Britain only six years earlier. Searching desperately for sources to raise the necessary funds, parliament accepted an initiative by William Paterson, a mostly unsuccessful entrepreneur and missionary,

---

24. Claydon, *William III and the Godly Revolution*, 26.

to found a bank to be designated the Bank of England.[25] The Bank was empowered by law to raise the necessary funds to pay for the outstanding costs of war with France, by means of a permanent loan secured on the country's future survival and prosperity. It was also allowed to issue promissory notes, that is to say paper currency, for the same sum as the loan, to be lent to entrepreneurs, and secured by the same interest on the country's future. All the money lent to the government was spent on the war. The only security for the interest on the loan, let alone the capital, was the future prosperity of the state, based on taxes raised or the resources of new lands yet to be exploited. But the new paper money was not secured against a pile of gold stashed away in the Bank's vaults. There was none. The new currency was debt. The bank lent debit notes, and those who borrowed and invested the money were simply trading with debt.

A statement by Philip Goodchild in his book *Theology of Money* exposes this trick at the heart of the Western banking system. The initial investors lent the *same* money to the state and to civil society. The loan to the latter was secured by the loan to the former in terms of future taxation. The security of the loan to the government was guaranteed in turn by economic growth in civil society. "It was a brilliant, self confirming system of mutual dependence and benefit."[26] The only new thing about trading with debt or toxic loans today is that these are doubly debt, for the money that finances the West already is debt. This makes sense of the current Western economic crisis and the huge bailouts of the banks. The Western economic system is entirely dependent on this hidden relationship between the state and the banks. If the banks fail, then the only hope for the state is to find a bigger, better bank, secured by a nation

25. See Mitchell, *Church, Gospel, & Empire*, 118–20.
26. Ibid., 10.

with better future chances of success and survival. It is for this reason that the biggest banks are now multi-national. But they need states, or perhaps eventually a one-world state, to survive.

Paterson drew overtly on messianic terminology and the idea of a neo-Israel theocratic state to justify the embryonic system. But behind his eschatological perspective lay, I suggest, at the deep structural level, Eusebius's soteriology of appeasement. It can be characterized as follows:

i. God created us in his hierarchical image of power and, when we broke his rules, was offended and meted out death and judgment to us.

ii. His offence and its retribution can only be met by payment in blood. Hence all the Jewish sacrifice system is seen as contributing to this appeasement, and Jesus' sacrifice on the cross is interpreted as the culmination of this. The payment reestablishes our measure of sovereign power in relation to his.

iii. This payment is mediated through a liturgy of obeisance by the church, above all in the eucharist. Eventually this transitions into the doctrine of transubstantiation where the sacrament becomes the actual body of Jesus. The Protestant once-and-for-all sacrifice fails to challenge this substantially. The priest or presbyter now makes this "currency" available to pay off God. The fullness of this payment will be realized in the heavenly kingdom to come.

iv. Now for priest or presbyter read banker, for sacrament read paper currency, and for heaven read future peace and prosperity of the nation state. The shift is total, and the underlying soteriology leads us relentlessly to the capitalism and biopower of today's West, as chapter 4 will continue to examine.

I want to make clear that I am not rejecting all sub-stitutionary ideas of the atonement here. In the book *Discovering Kenarchy*, the gospel testimony to the loving meaning and effect of the cross is considered in depth. It is the enduring idea of the cross as appeasement or pay-ment for God's offended sovereignty that I am highlighting and exposing as a corruption of the gospel testimony and a false myth in the deep structure of the Western system. The impact of this mistake on the testimony of Jesus, and the resilience of the loving good news despite it, is the subject of the next chapter.

3

The Progress of the Love Stream

(A) QUITE ANOTHER STORY

THE STORY OF THE partnership between church and empire begun in the previous chapter is incomplete without the seemingly subsidiary narrative of a stream of incarnational love that continued both within and alongside it. For while it is easy to demonstrate that the testimony to Jesus was displaced by the partnership, it does not follow that, from a divine perspective, God was at all nonplussed by it. Although the understanding of transcendence was severely damaged by the fall of the church and its subsequent effects, the divine nature portrayed in the gospel narrative was not so easily dislodged. Indeed, from the gospel perspective it would appear that God was used to adjusting to the insistent demands of human beings, particularly of his covenant people. Rather than giving up on them, his love moved him to persevere with them along paths which were clearly not his preferred route.

Jesus' view of himself and his teaching as the fullness of the Old Testament revelation bears this out. For example, in Matthew's account of the sermon on the mount, Jesus positions the Old Testament law only as the carrier of truth, not its completion.[1] Far from it in fact. For it turns out that for Jesus "an eye for an eye and a tooth for a tooth" was quite literally fulfilled by "turn the other cheek" and "love your enemies."[2] As the apostle Paul explains, in this way Jesus can be seen to fulfill the law by bringing it to an end.[3] Similarly, Jesus' understanding of himself as a king from David's line is utterly different to the Old Testament monarchy, with which it seems that God had become reluctantly associated,[4] and turns its hierarchical sovereignty and socio-economic status on its head.[5] To cap it all, his view of himself as the fulfillment of the temple involves its destruction as an earthly shrine and its resurrection as a body of people.[6]

Another way of reading all this is to see the Old Testament as the story of God's gift of himself to humanity in which, by act after act of self-emptying, he climbs into Israel's embrace of empire in its basic constructs of law, monarchy, and temple, none of which were his image for humanity. Looked at this way, the law was the replacement for covenant relationship, the monarchy for God's loving lordship, and the temple for his presence with his people everywhere. If we read the Old Testament story of Abraham and Isaac from the same perspective, it casts important light on the controlling appeasement myth of empire underlying

1. Matt 5:17.
2. Matt 5:38–44.
3. Rom 10:4.
4. 1 Sam 8:1–22.
5. Luke 20:41–44.
6. John 2:19–22.

all three of these basic structures. God's invitation to Abraham to sacrifice his son is positioned as the revelation that God is the one who steps into the terrible consequences of the appeasement myth. God does this, not in order to reinforce empire, but to undo it and reveal the kenotic nature of his loving power at the heart of the creation. The lamb that he famously provides at the eleventh hour stands for God himself, not an appeasement victim.[7]

This revelation comes to its zenith in the gospel story. God doesn't need or want appeasement because he takes all the consequences of human sin himself. This counter-imperial interpretation of divine activity has two crucial implications. Firstly, sin is not framed as the behavior that offends sovereign power, but as a self-centered, overbearing attitude towards the creation, God himself, and the image of the Trinity in other human beings. Sin is seen as that which insists on its own way, despoils love and breaks relationship. Secondly, God's positioning as the ram caught in the thicket and ready to be sacrificed, accounts for the way that God continually appears to step into the consequences of humanity's fallen choices and exhaust them in himself. It finds its culmination in the incarnation, cross, and resurrection where God identifies with sin and its results and is proved the victor.

Such a way of interpreting the Old Testament in the light of the gospel testimony suggests a parallel response in the context of the fall of the church. It would follow that, far from rejecting the church and the empire it embraced, God would choose to remain within it once again, continually manifesting himself alongside the trajectory of sovereign power with a counterpolitical kenarchy. I am using this word "counterpolitical" to signify a politics that runs counter to the underlying accepted order, or status quo.

7. Gen 22:7–13.

This kind of politics is "counterpolitics," with its adjective "counterpolitical." Kenarchy, because it is a way of relating to people that runs counter to the status quo, or what I have termed the "currency" of sovereignty, is counterpolitical. With this in mind, we will now explore some situations in the history of the church, which I unearthed during my research into the currency of sovereignty discussed in the preceding chapter, and consider their significance as evidence of this kind of response.

(B) REVIVALS OF THE LOVE STREAM

(1) Unity in diversity

The first of these manifestations of the love stream comes from Eusebius's own *History of the Church*[8] where he tells the stories of Irenaeus and Dionysius, two early church leaders who resolved controversies over baptism and the date of Easter that, if handled differently, would have tended towards the reemergence of the law-monarchy-temple system. They are extremely significant stories because the loving, kenotic approach taken in each case pointed the way to the submission of opinion to relationship without devaluing its content. Unbeknown to Irenaeus and Dionysius themselves, their loving example provided the basis for the resolution of what could have been moments of subversive spirituality at crucial points yet to come in the history of the West. In Irenaeus's case it was the matter of the date of Easter. As Eusebius describes, in the late second century, Victor, "the head of the Roman church," was excommunicating whole dioceses because they did not keep Easter in the same way as he recommended. Irenaeus's

8. Eusebius, *The History of the Church*, 180–81.

response is very significant, for he was not legalistic about it at all, being of the opinion that "the divergency in the fast emphasizes the unanimity of our faith."[9] In contrast with those who initiated the later debate on the question at the church councils of Nicaea and Whitby, he resolved it in the interests of a unity in diversity that honored difference and protected the validity of alternative standpoints.[10] The Nicaea and Whitby debates, on the other hand, were resolved in the cause of uniformity and monarchical control. They led to one of the deepest and most acrimonious divisions in medieval Christianity.

For Dionysius the issue was the matter of rebaptism, which arose in a time of persecution when people were required to deny the faith at threat of death.[11] Faced with this, some did deny their faith, and the question arose as to whether those who denied their faith under duress could be rebaptized and thereby reinstated in the church community. In Africa, rebaptism was practiced although it was disapproved of in the Eastern church. Dionysius displayed a loving flexibility towards his African friends, despite his own reservations about their practice. Had his example been followed by Zwingli and the early Swiss reformers, the murder of Felix Manz and the other Anabaptist advocates of rebaptism, whom they deliberately drowned in Lake Zurich, would never have occurred. A centuries-long rift between radical Christians resulting in extraordinarily painful displacements of population would have been averted.[12]

9. Ibid., 232.

10. Mitchell, *Church, Gospel, & Empire*, 46.

11. Ibid., 47.

12. http://en.wikipedia.org/wiki/Felix_Manz.

(2) Reconfiguring the church

By the late twelfth century, as we have seen, Pope Innocent III and the Holy Roman Emperor Frederick II were busy strengthening the currency of power, law, and payment in both church and empire. At the same time and in the same geographical and political contexts, Joachim of Fiore and Francis of Assisi were pioneering new ways of thinking and being the church. Joachim was a courageous and prophetic innovator in thought and practice who recognized the need for a complete reconfiguration of both the structure of the church and the way its history had generally been understood.[13] Born around 1135, he had several formative spiritual encounters during a visit to Palestine. After a diplomatic career he joined the Benedictines but later separated from them to found the order of St Giovanni in Fiore in 1196. He died in 1202.

Joachim developed an exciting approach to history that drew on the relationships within the Trinity to present a progressive understanding of God's relationship with his people. He saw history as overlapping periods during which the influence of the Father, the Son, or the Holy Spirit was particularly prominent. The effect was to provide a radical view of God's work within and alongside the partnership of church and empire. He understood the monastic movement from Benedict onwards as a whole new age or dispensation of the Spirit. As a result, instead of swapping the true body of Christ for the sacrament like his compatriots, as we saw in the previous chapter, he presented the new monasticism as a restoration of the true body of Christ. His prophecies positioned the emperor Frederick II as the Antichrist and Francis of Assisi's new movement as a fulfillment of the new dispensation of the Spirit.

13. See Mitchell, *Church, Gospel, & Empire*, 87–90.

If only Joachim's own plans for the new monastic order could have reflected Jesus' egalitarian approach and moved beyond a dependence on hierarchy and approval by the papacy, a counterpolitical shift might have taken place on which Francis of Assisi and his new monastic movement could have built. A radical model might have been provided for reformers to take the church in a direction leading to a very different future for the West. However, his innovative interpretation of history and his new monasticism remained stubbornly wedded to the need for a hierarchical father both in the monastery and in the church at large. As a result, his intended dispensation of the Spirit continued to legitimate the sovereign currency of the West. His innovative dispensationalism, or way of understanding history as a series of strategic time periods, eventually became synonymous with an eschatology that affirmed the status quo, right down to the *Left Behind* series of books and films.[14] There is, of course, no reason why this should be the necessary outcome of Joachim's innovative dispensational approach, which was radical in its initial impact on both church and empire.

Similarly, in the case of Francis, his emphasis on those aspects of the gospel story that embraced the multitude of the poor marked an alternative direction from the twelfth-century mystification of the true body of Christ. Instead, his monastic practice or *rule* centered around the attempt to order daily life on the counterpolitical lordship of Jesus as encountered in the gospel narratives. The effect of this was the introduction of the initial stages of an economy of gift in contrast to the prevailing currency of empire.[15] Francis was an exceptional innovator. His progress to absolute poverty

14. A series of sixteen best-selling novels by Tim LaHaye and Jerry B. Jenkins and the films based on them.

15. Ibid., 90–94.

centered around three prophetic experiences. The first was a dream that led him to reject military weaponry and turn back from enlisting in Innocent III's business of the cross. This was followed by a vision which personalized Poverty as a woman that he was marrying, as a result of which he became absorbed with the issue of poverty. Finally, there was his experience at the decaying church of St Damian when he heard the words "Francis, go, repair my house."

These spiritual experiences and Francis's responses to them struck at the heart of the currency of sovereignty in terms of power, law, and payment. Turning back from his journey to enlist in Pope Innocent's "holy" war, his response was to take the cloth from his father's shop and sell it to provide building materials for the ruined church. When the church authorities insisted that he must return his father's property as it was not right that the church benefit from money to which it was not legally entitled, he stripped himself naked publicly and returned the money for the cloth together with his own clothes stating, "from now on I will say 'Our Father who art in heaven,' and not Father Peter Bernadone" (his own father). By this powerful act he seemed to be stripping himself, and the church that he set out to rebuild, from the partnership of church and empire. Not only did he reject dependence on military power and the social and familial authority of the law, but also reliance on money and property. In response to Christ's call to follow without money, food, shoes, or extra clothes, he declared, "this is what I want to do with all my heart."[16] Despite relying on begging for support, his rule rejected all laziness and required the deployment of practical skills and manual labor by his followers. The resultant order offered a profound counterpolitical reengagement with society, spreading rapidly and involving many lay people. As

16. Ibid., 91.

Paul Sabatier claims, "it was a social revolution."[17] This is confirmed by the social alignment achieved when Francis intervened in the political affairs of Assisi. The agreed *pace civile* stated: "Without common consent there shall never be any sort of alliance either with the pope and his nuncios or legates, or with the emperor, or with the king . . . or with any city or town, or with any important person."[18]

This new egalitarianism marked Francis's relationships with his fellow friars. His non-hierarchical approach was demonstrated by giving others the lead and relinquishing it altogether long before his death. It was also in evidence in his close relationship with his colleague Clare, who founded her own partner order. They gladly lived among social rejects and lepers and declared that God delighted to be with the outcasts of the world and with the simple. This, together with his radical rejection of money and private property, pointed away from the gospel as payment to the gospel as kenotic gift. However, despite influencing the church's refusal of usury for several centuries, his tendency to romanticize his "Lady Poverty" and his strong affirmation of the new transubstantiation that made the eucharist into the actual body of Jesus, worked directly against this kenotic potential in the end. Otherwise it could have gone a long way towards proving that an economy of gift could be an alternative to the currency of sovereignty and the capitalism in which it culminated.

(3) Digging deep

The characters described in the chapter so far are examples of the flow of the love stream on the inside of the partnership of church and empire. In the decades leading up to the

17. Sabatier, *Life of St Francis of Assisi*, 56.
18. See Mitchell, *Gospel, Church, & Empire*, 92.

culmination of the appeasement motif in the debt-based currency of the Bank of England, a whole raft of radical experiments away from the currency of empire took place. This was a time of such great conflict and upheaval between the old universal forms of sovereignty and the newly emerging multiplied forms that cracks formed in the body politic. These were so deep as to allow newly erupting currents of the love stream to spring up outside the partnership altogether. In Britain during the middle years of the seventeenth century these eruptions were of such seismic proportions that those who dug the wells from which they sprang, made the naive, if understandable, assumption that their endeavors really would overcome the oppressions of Christendom.

Two British pioneers, Gerrard Winstanley and William Penn, particularly illustrate the depths to which the stream penetrated at this time, and its possibilities for the future. While Joachim and Francis had attempted to reshape the church and its theology from the inside, these two successors dug down to the very foundations of the Western system. They ventured even to challenge the generally accepted assumptions about the relationship between people and property. In the accepted currency of sovereignty the ultimate sovereign power was God, who owned everything in consequence of his ultimate might. His delegated next in line, the emperor, similarly owned it all as his representative. He demonstrated his right to land and property by violence or the threat of it. This possession in fact (*de facto*) was then made into possession by law (*de jure*). Once sovereignty was multiplied, it followed that those who had now obtained a limited degree of sovereignty must hold a parallel amount of property, similarly protected by law and, if necessary, enforced by violence and war. Hence the need to find a means of providing and protecting property for the newly multiplying sovereign powers, that the new Bank of England epitomized and legalized.

Winstanley and Penn, and others like them, dared to excavate the very basis of the relationship between God, people, land, and property. Whereas Francis of Assisi had renounced his own possessions and embraced poverty, his reliance on begging for support still left him dependent on the existing funds of church and empire. In fact, the two senior clerics with whom Francis built the closest relationships were Bishop Guido, the richest landowner in Assisi and a fierce defender of his power and riches against the civil authorities, and Cardinal Ugolino of Ostia, later Pope Gregory IX, who became protector of the fraternity and did not hesitate to use the friars to defend the church and its authority.[19] So while the personal practice of Francis and his followers emulated the gospel testimony to a degree, it failed to challenge the dependence of the institutional church and state political structure on private property. The gospel testimony, however, was unequivocal in its application to all disciples. As Luke's narrative has it, "none of you can be My disciple who does not give up all his own possessions."[20] My point here is not that the gospel favors absolute poverty, or in any way devalues the gift of creation, but rather that the language and example of the Jesus story advocates stewardship, not ownership. The examples of Luke's account of the rich young ruler and Zaccheus, together with his Acts account of the story of Ananias and Sapphira, bear this out.[21] The point seems to be that whatever a disciple has is to be stewarded as a counterpolitical resource to release to others, as the Holy Spirit leads. Viewed in this light, Winstan-

19. Robson, *St Francis of Assisi, The Legend and the Life*, 31, 42, 117, 126.

20. Luke 14:33.

21. Luke 18:22–24; 19:8; Acts 5:1–4.

ley's and Penn's experiments with the land struck at the very foundations of empire.

Gerard Winstanley was probably born in Wigan in 1609 and moved to London as a clothing apprentice.[22] He prospered in his work, becoming a freeman of the Merchant Taylors Company in 1637. However, a combination of high taxation and trade depression brought him into financial difficulties, which caused him to leave London for the Cobham area of Surrey. At this time he believed that he heard God speaking to him in a vision the words, "Worke together, Eat bread together; declare this all abroad." He interpreted this as a divine invitation to a corporate stewardship of God's gift of the creation in what he saw as a new moment of opportunity. In January 1649, the same year as the execution of King Charles I, he published the pamphlet *The New Law of Righteousness Budding Forth to Restore the Whole Creation from Bondage of the Curse.* Joining together with the prophetic company of William Everard and half a dozen or so others, on Sunday April 8 Winstanley set about digging and planting vegetables on common land at St George's Hill near Cobham.

They and others like them became known as the Diggers because of their practice of combining digging up common land for the benefit of the poor and dispossessed, with digging deeply into contemporary thought and politics. During the week following, they returned in increasing numbers and began burning off the heath in preparation for growing grain. By the weekend they were at Kingston market buying corn and inviting all the poor to come and help them, with the promise of food, drink, and clothing in return. It is important to understand that "common" land, at least since the Norman invasion, was not commonly

22. For more background and reference sources for Gerard Winstanley, see Mitchell, *Gospel, Church, & Empire,* 125–26.

owned, but belonged to the landowners of the manors in which it lay. The tenants of these landlords held specific shared rights "in common" on it, for which they paid rents and dues. The Diggers argued that this whole feudal system had rested on theft and forcible seizure, but had come to an end with the execution of Charles. They were non-violent, peaceful people, as their songs make clear and in particular this stanza against the monarchists highlights:

> To conquer them by love,
> come in now, come in now
> To conquer them by love, come in now;
> To conquer them by love, as itt does you behove,
> For hee is King above, noe power is like to love,
> Glory heere, Diggers all.[23]

Neighboring landowners, the landlords of the manors themselves, and those stirred up on their behalf rightly regarded the Diggers' actions as an attack on private property as a whole. Amid appeals to the new Commonwealth military leadership, they harassed the Diggers with increasing violence. As a result, the "budding forth" of the Diggers' new order on St George's Hill lasted barely a year, after which Winstanley appears to have settled back into a more conventional style of life. Nevertheless, his courage and uncompromising writings earned him a place alongside Marx and Engels on the first monument of the Russian Revolution erected by Lenin in 1918.

The plight of the Diggers under Cromwell's Commonwealth is evidence of what Giorgio Agamben has described as the emergence of the sovereignty of "the People." While the root meaning of "hierarchy" is simply order itself, in the centuries of partnership between church and empire, as chapter 2 makes clear, it had come to carry the unavoidable sense of graded rank, with the monarch at the top, next to

23. http://www.diggers.org/diggers/digg_eb.html.

God, and the people beneath, as in the political theology of Eusebius and his successors. The republican order also subjugated the people, but this time through leaders who ruled via a legal framework where the people were ranked under the sovereignty of "the People." In this context Agamben helpfully distinguishes "the people" as the excluded multitude from "the People" as sovereign power.[24] So the power wielded by Oliver Cromwell was not, as it proved, very different from that wielded by Charles I, despite the king's removal. The struggle had been between the emerging multiplied sovereignty of the bourgeoisie and merchant landowners in parliament, and the superior claims of divine right by the monarch and those aristocrats and others who supported him. With his execution, the sovereignty simply passed to the new representatives of the People, who did little to change the situation of the dispossessed and the poor.

While Winstanley was digging up St George's Hill, William Penn was just five years old. Penn was an exact contemporary of Gilbert Burnet, the pioneer of the new multiplied sovereignty described in the previous chapter. Son of the wealthy Vice-Admiral Sir William Penn and his wife Mary, the extraordinary times in which Penn grew up had a profound effect on him. At only twelve, while contemplating the turbulence and injustice of his time, he had a profoundly transcendent encounter that led him to conclude that he was being called by God. He was a student at Oxford when in 1661 the Corporation Act required all municipal officers to participate in the sacraments of the established church, and the Act of Uniformity obligated all clergy to the Book of Common Prayer. In 1662 the Quaker Act made it illegal for Quakers to gather in groups of more than five members. This did not sit well with Penn's direct experience

24. Agamben, *Means Without End. Notes on Politics*, 8–34.

of God and he made no secret of it. By the time he was eighteen he had already been expelled from Cambridge for being too religious and a non-conformist. Physically beaten and sent by his father to Paris in the company of exemplary young noblemen for two years, in hope of distancing him from his non-conformist contacts and experiences, Penn afterwards spent a brief period studying law before being sent off to manage the family estates in Ireland. However, here he reencountered the Quaker preacher Thomas Loe, whom he had heard while at Cambridge, and consequently went through a defining conversion, embracing the Quaker way of life. Penn soon became a traveling evangelist and prolific writer in the Quaker cause of personal faith and religious and political freedom.

By mid December 1668, when Burnet was being appointed Professor of Divinity in Glasgow, Penn was languishing in the Tower of London for publishing *The Sandy Foundation Shaken*, a pamphlet challenging the established order and defending freedom of conscience. He was eventually released through the influence of his father, the following July. In prison again in 1670 and 1674 and faced with ongoing persecution, Penn and his fellow Quakers began to pursue the possibility of establishing a colony of their own in America. But theirs was to be no ordinary colony where the colonists simply took over the land and ruled as the superior power, killing or subduing the indigenous peoples. Instead Penn was determined to steward the land together with its native inhabitants. William's father had lent King Charles II substantial sums of money to help fund the consolidation of the monarchy during the Restoration period. With his death, the king was indebted to Penn in the amount of £16,000, in those days a huge sum that he could not afford to pay. So when Penn formally petitioned Charles for a grant of land in the New World in 1680, the king saw the possibility of discharging his debt and getting rid of the Quakers in one move. Penn found himself, at the age of thirty-six, according to the sovereign law of England, the sole proprietor of twenty-eight million acres of what is now Pennsylvania.

Penn immediately embarked on what he described as a "holy experiment."[25] At the heart of this was the seed of what was to become the American Constitution, and a fledgling state council put together in a series of unique treaties concluding with the Great Treaty of 1683. By means of these treaties, Penn, entirely unarmed, recognized the Delaware as the host inhabitants and owners of Pennsylvania, paid them for the privilege of joint stewardship of the greater part of what is now south-eastern Pennsylvania for the mutual, loving cohabitation of the two peoples, and included the Delaware in the state council. In contrast to the small Digger colony on St George's Hill, this territory was vast and the experiment lasted for seventy years until his descendants broke the terms of the Great Treaty and the Native Americans were excluded both from the council and their own land. Had Penn's experiment succeeded beyond his generation, Pennsylvania might today still be a collaborative stewardship of the land and its resources between the incoming Europeans and the Delaware. Had the experiment continued and been maintained throughout the later developments of the American Constitution, the whole United States might have provided the basis for an alternative model for Western politics.

Since these experiments, there have of course been many attempts, both within and alongside the church and nation state in the West, to take initiatives to revolutionize the relationship between people and land. In the last

25. For a full treatment of this, see Fields with Fields, *The Seed of a Nation.*

hundred years these have been against the broader background of the communist experiments extending beyond or outside the West as in the former USSR, China, Cuba, and North Korea. These are examples of socialist sovereignty rather than capitalist sovereignty, either in a version of the old universal model under a totalitarian leader, or as examples of the sovereignty of the People over the people. What is clear in terms of the currency of sovereignty put forward in this book, is that these political systems are all part of a sovereignty "set" and as such are not so different from the sovereignty of the West as we are generally inclined to believe. As far as the radical innovations in the politics of land and property within the West are concerned, the cooperative societies, friendly societies, allotment associations, and allied experiments in the collaborative stewardship of land and property have provided good examples of the direction in which future experiments might yet take us. One of the most realistic and successful has been the reclamation of the Scottish island of Eigg by its inhabitants, chronicled by Alastair McIntosh in his book *Soil and Soul*.[26] Recently, bold experiments like the Todmorton[27] initiative where the planting of food crops at forty public locations throughout the town offers locals, and visitors, the chance to pick their own fresh fruit and vegetables free of charge, show what can be achieved with publicly held land. The companion volume will attempt to evaluate the politics of Jesus with regard to land and property and apply it to contemporary issues in more detail. Suffice it to point out that such are the ongoing effects of the partnership of church and empire that even today in the United Kingdom 70 percent of the

26. McIntosh, *Soil and Soul: People versus Corporate Power*.

27. http://www.agriculturesnetwork.org/magazines/global/regional-food-systems/edible-todmorden.

land is still owned by 1 percent of the people.[28] On the wider scale, only 15 percent of the world's population own any land at all.

The dislocation of the multitude from the land and its resources is ironically both an indictment of the idea of peace through sovereignty and the means to its success. For it has been the separation of the multitude from the raw materials of subsistence that land represents that has allowed the powerful few to control the means of production and amass the resources necessary to the imperial project through which the imagined peace comes. This situation, however, is changing dramatically as the Western system comes to what Foucault and others have described as its biopolitical fullness, or biopower. For in the contemporary postmodern world the progress of peace through sovereign power that drives the Western economic system is culminating in the commodification of human life itself. In the Greek language the word for life is *bios*, hence the development of the words "biopower" and "biopolitics" to refer to this phenomenon. This process is bringing the plight of the multitude to a climax in an extraordinary way. The problem is no longer that so many are separated from the raw material of subsistence and production. Now they themselves have become the raw material. This twenty-first-century development in the human condition is both a new slavery and yet a new opportunity for change like never before. It is this opportunity, and the new availability of egalitarian grace to meet it, that the next chapter investigates.

28. Cowley, "The coming battle over land and property."

4

Biopower Meets the Holy Spirit

(A) THE COMMODIFICATION OF LIFE ITSELF

BIOPOWER IS THE WORD coined by the French philosopher
Michel Foucault to refer to the commodification of life itself.[1] It refers to the way in which the everyday experiences of human life, together with the skills and capabilities of
human beings, have now become the raw material of commerce necessary to the ongoing existence of the Western
world and the economic system on which it depends. This
raw material or *bios* has been described by other writers as
"naked life" and "bare life," to underline the way in which
the economic system has moved beyond dependency on
the use of human skills and capabilities, or what Marx
called labor power, and now utilizes the essential experience of living: human psychology, sexuality, physical
health, affections, relationships, and so on. You can see this

1. For a full coverage of the significance of the term, cf. *Church,
Gospel, & Empire*, 131–51.

happening in various types of work. For example, in industrial production, information networks transform the production process which, instead of driving the market, now interfaces and communicates with it. In interactive work, such as computerized tailoring or weaving, symbolic analysis and problem solving are increasingly interposed between the worker and their product. Then in the health services and entertainment, sensory experiences of healing or pleasure are provided, but on leaving the hospital or cinema, for example, there are no materially measurable outcomes apart from those feelings. Or to put it another way, the personal sphere as well as the social sphere is now the focus and the material of economic production.

The concept of biopower carries with it the claim that there is no longer any personal or private sphere unaffected by or outside the influence of the market. A corollary of this is that capitalism no longer depends on external factors to make it work, but the drive is now contained within the system itself. Through the influence of the news media, television, and film, together with the all-pervading economic orientation of politics, education, and culture generally, human beings are embedded in a worldview that assumes the primacy of profit in everything. For this reason Foucault refers to the postmodern biopolitical world as the society of control. This control is not immediately obvious to us even while we are experiencing it, because we are on the inside of the system. Rather, it needs exposing and explaining to us. It is often only after the shock of realization brought about by counterpolitical films such as the *Matrix* trilogy and *Inception*, or the philosophical writing of thinkers like Giorgio Agamben, who likens today's Western society to a prison camp, that we begin to understand what is happening.

For those with eyes to see, ever since the banking crisis of 2008, the economic repercussions have been revealing the strength and depth of this interior control exercised by the market. It is assumed by the benefactors of the system that sweeping reductions in social provision and austerity cuts on care for the disabled, poor, and vulnerable are simply the necessary costs of the huge bailouts that had to be made to prevent the complete collapse of the banks and to recover economic equilibrium. But instead the cuts are really exposing the inherent weakness of the system itself, which is dependent on the sovereignty of the rich and the powerful to function. As a result, the financial cuts and economic savings that are being made primarily benefit the wealthy at the expense of the poor. Nevertheless, with the passage of time, it is becoming increasingly obvious that the debt-based financial system that has transitioned from the partnership of church and empire has now colonized not only the poor, but human existence itself. So although it is still the poor that suffer, it is a suffering that is spreading rapidly throughout the whole system. When life itself is the raw material, all of life is eaten up. Rich as well as poor soon become the victims of the voracious market.

But at the same time two remarkable parallel facts apply. Firstly, because human emotions and relationships have been added to theoretical knowledge and practical skills as the raw material at the heart of the system, the opportunity for reflection and evaluation is more generally accessible across the whole of life. The Internet and the technical innovations that go with it such as computers, mobile phones, and iPads place emotional and social intelligence at the center of the commercial communication process alongside rational and theoretical intelligence. As a result the whole range of human potentiality now lies at the heart of the market system. While it takes time for the possibilities provided by this to dawn, it means that the system is arguably more vulnerable to human desires for fundamental change than ever before in its history. This has huge eschatological implications, for it means that biopower is right now carrying the seeds of its own destruction. The Western economic system, birthed out of the partnership of church and empire, appears to be coming to a final crisis at last. Thinkers like Hardt and Negri are beginning to perceive this capacity for biopower to provide for its own dissolution. From their perspective, only one thing is lacking to activate this, and that is the practical motivation to reimagine and embrace another way to peace for humankind and our planet. In order to achieve this, despite the record of the Christendom partnership, they have the prophetic insight to call for a reconsideration of Judeo-Christian love. "Christianity and Judaism . . . both conceive love as a political act that constructs the multitude . . . We need to recover today this material and political sense of love, a love as strong as death."[2]

The second parallel fact, at least from an incarnational perspective, is that because our very life is the fuel of the system, and because as well as material entities we are spiritual beings, then the human spirit is also at the heart of biopower, and can be exercised to break free of it. The clear statement of Jesus, according to John's gospel, bears this out: "It is the Spirit who gives life; the flesh profits nothing."[3] Given that humans are spiritual beings, capable of apprehending transcendence, then the availability of the loving Spirit of Jesus means that it is possible to resource this breakthrough. The difficulty for those who have rejected transcendence because they see it as the cause and carrier of sovereign power, is how to reengage the necessary degree of love to achieve the mobilization of the multitude. While Hardt and Negri are at pains to point out that love does not need a metaphysical worldview to justify it, the

2. Hardt and Negri, *Multitude*, 352.

3. John 6:63.

issue is not so much the worldview, but the depth of unconditional love required to break through the all-pervading sovereignty of the many generations of Western tradition. Yet, were this motivation and energy in place, then the human spiritual potential inherent within biopower might be used to instigate a whole new means to peace beyond sovereignty. Although thinkers such as Agamben doubt the possibility of this ever happening without default back to sovereign power, the naked transcendence revealed in the voluntary embrace of victimhood by the life, death, and resurrection of Jesus meets this doubt with unsubsumed egalitarian transcendence. For if the transcendent creator became immanent in Jesus inside the imperial system to undo it, we can say that while this kind of transcendence did not purpose the partnership of church and empire that followed, it has remained with us in it.

(B) ANOTHER FULLNESS OF TIMES

Chapter 2 has already considered the way that the colonization of transcendence by sovereignty at the height of the Caesar cult was met by the counterpolitics of the Jesus story. It is one of the most hopeful portents of our times that the culmination of the genealogy of church and empire is met once again by a new fullness of unsubsumed transcendence. I refer to the initial phases of the twentieth-century Pentecostal-Charismatic movement, the socio-political implications of which have until recently largely been overlooked by Western commentators. Nevertheless, the exponential growth of the movement means that it is impossible to ignore it any longer. Current statistics give the number of Pentecostal-Charismatic Christians as more than 614 million,[4] consisting therefore of approximately one

4. Johnson, *The Global Dynamics of the Pentecostal and*

in eleven of the current population of the world. They can be found in 9,000 ethno-linguistic cultures, speaking 8,000 languages,[5] now extending mainly beyond the boundaries of the West. As Philip Jenkins surmises, "One way or another, inside the Catholic Church or outside it, Third World Christianity is becoming steadily more Pentecostal."[6] Chapter 1 has already explained the connection as well as the polarization between the secular and sacred in contemporary society. It is now time to explore the relationship between these two perspectives with regard to biopower and what Vinson Synan has called "The Century of the Holy Spirit."[7] But before proceeding to do so, it is necessary to remind ourselves of the initial egalitarian character of the three main recognized Pentecostal-Charismatic outpourings of the twentieth century.

(1) Three generations of Pentecostal outpouring

(a) Azusa Street

Almost all the many expressions of the Pentecostal-Charismatic movement recognize the ecstatic experiences of the 1906 Los Angeles Azusa Street revival as one of the most important defining narratives. Peter Hocken makes clear in his recent comprehensive overview of the material that "when we examine Pentecostalism as a historically identifiable movement, then the evidence does point to . . . Azusa Street playing a major role in the identity and diffusion of the movement."[8] From the start, this experience of the pres-

---

Charismatic Renewal, 482.

    5. Barrett, "The Worldwide Holy Spirit Renewal," 383.

    6. Jenkins, *The Next Christendom*, 67.

    7. Synan, *The Century of the Holy Spirit*.

    8. Hocken, *The Challenges of the Pentecostal, Charismatic and*

ence of God was overwhelmingly egalitarian. I am using the word egalitarian here to refer to those circumstances in which an equal opportunity for recognition and engagement is given to all humans involved, irrespective of gender, rank, or race.[9]

The *Los Angeles Times* of April 18, 1906 famously records meetings in what is described as a tumble-down shack. "On Azusa Street, near San Pedro Street . . . colored people and a sprinkling of whites compose the congregation, and night is made hideous in the neighborhood by the howlings of the worshipers who spend hours swaying forth and back in a nerve-racking [*sic*] attitude of prayer and supplication. They claim to have the 'gift of tongues,' and to be able to comprehend the babel." Frank Bartleman, a journalist personally involved in the events, describes them from the perspective of a participant: "Divine love was wonderfully manifest in the meetings. They would not even allow an unkind word said against their opposers, or the churches. The message was the love of God. It was a sort of 'first love' of the early church returned. The 'baptism' as we received it in the beginning did not allow us to think, speak, or hear evil of any man."[10] Accounts are unanimous that a countercultural, non-hierarchical unity of male and female, black and white, rich and poor, characterized the embryonic movement.[11] While William Seymour, a second-generation African-American slave descendant, was clearly recognized

---

Messianic Jewish Movements, 19.

9. A Western, rights-based definition is being avoided because such rights are sovereignty and law based, and therefore work against egalitarianism in the end.

10. Bartleman, *Azusa Street*, 54.

11. Synan, *The Century of the Holy Spirit*, 49, 54–55; Wacker, *Heaven Below*, 104–5; Hepden, "The Impact of Racial Inclusivity in the Azusa Street Revival."

as the nominal leader, there was no structured hierarchy. "We had no priest class, nor priest craft . . . We did not even have a platform or a pulpit in the beginning. All were on a level."[12] This paralleled the developing labor movement, predated women's suffrage by more than a decade,[13] and preceded racial equality by more than half a century.[14] The Jim Crow laws had been in effect at Charles Parham's Apostolic Faith Bible School in Houston where Seymour had been obliged to listen to Parham's teachings about the Holy Spirit outside the classroom through an open door. But in Frank Bartleman's words, in the subsequent ecstatic events of 1906 "the color line was washed away in the blood."[15]

At the outset, the movement recognized the radical political implications of this egalitarian harmony and its distinction from the nation state which depended on law, war, and money to bring peace. Parham, one of the most universally recognized, although ambivalent Pentecostal leaders, who early on struggled with the social diversity of the Azusa Street happenings, nonetheless "consistently resisted any hint of dual allegiance to the Kingdom of God and that of Caesar."[16] Long before the outbreak of war within Europe he berated all so-called Christian nation states, including the United States, for yielding themselves up to the "Moloch God, Patriotism, whose doctrine was honor," whose soldiers were "self-appointed murderers," and whose governments were "imbecile."[17] The Azusa Street experience, and the many similar expressions of divine presence

12. Bartleman, *Azusa Street*, 57.

13. Women did not get the vote in the US until 1919.

14. This was the height of the era of the Jim Crow laws of racial segregation.

15. Bartleman, *Azusa Street*, 54.

16. Wacker, *Heaven Below*, 218.

17. Ibid., 218.

that ensued, facilitated a resurgence of the multitude of ordinary people beyond the growing biopolitical control of sovereignty and money. This is clear both from the many popular biographies and testimonies from Frank Bartleman onwards, as well as the evidence of the growing confidence of third-world Pentecostalism as the church of the poor.[18]

(b) The mid and late twentieth-century Charismatic outpourings

While the racial make-up of the initial mid-century Charismatic visitation was admittedly more uniform, owing in part to the lost opportunities of the season that preceded it, as we shall see shortly, the egalitarian nature remained. As the characteristic direction of the movement was into the institutional and long-established churches and denominations, the events took place among both clergy and laity. But the trend was unmistakable; it was from the grassroots outwards. As popular accounts of the experiences, such as Dennis Bennett's *Nine O'clock in the Morning*, make clear, the clergy generally experienced the outpouring through the laity or junior clergy.[19] The initial context was usually ordinary homes, not official church buildings.[20] The impact among the poor, particularly in the non-Western continents, is a defining characteristic.[21] The transcendence was once again initially egalitarian and unsubsumed.

It is true that the third generation of outpouring was initiated by spiritual hunger among existing leaders, either among the laity or in the context of existing Charismatic

18. Ma, "When the Poor are Fired Up," 28–34.

19. Bennett, *Nine O'clock in the Morning*, 157.

20. Ibid., 20.

21. Hollenweger, "The Pentecostal Elites and the Pentecostal Poor," 201, 205.

churches and movements.[22] However, it was as a participant in these more recent outpourings of the 1990s that I was first alerted to the initial egalitarian nature of divine grace in all three of these Pentecostal outpourings of the last century. I was privileged to have first-hand experience of the eighty days of outpouring in the Ichthus Fellowship in Greenwich, South East London, the Toronto Airport Christian Fellowship outpouring in Mississauga and Toronto, Canada, and the antecedent events of the Argentinean Revival. However hard we tried to protect ourselves, the distinctive manifestations of these moves invariably targeted and humbled hierarchical positions, ranks, offices, and behaviors.

(2) Giving in to empire

Although the initial visitations of the Pentecostal-Charismatic movement were so clearly egalitarian, the deep-seated mindsets of the church-empire partnership proved extraordinarily resistant to change, which had a serious impact on the shape of church and ministry beyond the initial stages of each of the three generations of renewal, allowing aspects of subsumed transcendence into the ensuing visitations. This tendency to accommodate to the prevailing politics of the day is described by Grant Wacker as Pentecostal "pragmatism," in contrast to the earlier egalitarian experience, which he describes as "primitivism."[23] It helps account for the way that the movement tended to support the expressions of church and state of twentieth-century America, beginning with attempts to consolidate the originary transcendent Pentecostal experiences into the constituted structures of denominations and networks. Over time the experimental initiatives and communities were either

22. See, for example, Arnott, *The Father's Blessing,* 57–59.

23. Wacker, *Heaven Below,* 226.

absorbed into existing holiness denominations, for example the Church of God, the Pentecostal Holiness Church, and the Church of God in Christ, or developed into completely new ecclesial structures and networks like the Assemblies of God, the Pentecostal Assemblies of the World, and the United Pentecostal Church.[24] To begin with, these tried to maintain the purity of the originary expressions of reconciling love, but before long the ecclesial expressions began to betray evidence of the familiar sovereign forms. The operation of authority remained generally hierarchical, whether Presbyterian or Episcopalian or New Apostolic, and a significant part of the theology of God and salvation, which provided the focus of worship and liturgy, continued to carry the familiar imperial version of the salvation story. All of this meant that the developing movement was less than able to provide the radical counterpolitical activism that each new stage of the outpouring warranted.

One of the first evidences of this failure was the social subjugation and segregation of African-Americans. The racial equality evident in the primitive beginnings eventually gave way to the racism inherent in the American church and society at the beginning of the twentieth century. As a result, by 1914 Seymour had decided to restrict directors' posts at the Azusa Mission to "people of Color," and by the mid twenties two of the most significant interracial groupings, the Pentecostal Assemblies of the World and the Church of God in Christ, followed the politics of the day and divided along racial lines.[25] Wacker emphasizes racism as the first of three foci at the heart of the move towards pragmatism, to which he adds recourse to the law and a sustained loyalty to the American pilgrim dream.[26] From

24. Synan, *The Century of the Holy Spirit*, 5–6.

25. Wacker, *Heaven Below*, 231.

26. Ibid., 226.

the perspective of this book it was the partnership of church and empire that lay behind that dream. Racism can then be seen as part and parcel of the process towards sovereignty, where those of another race or culture are relegated further down the hierarchy of relative power.

The recourse to law formed the second pragmatic accommodation to the political configurations of empire. It is clear from the *Los Angeles Times* report on Azusa Street that the immediacy of the Pentecostals' spiritual encounters could appear anti-social to their neighbors. The interpretation of their experience as the restoration of the Holy Spirit to the world in preparation for the return of Christ made their testimony and subsequent evangelism urgent and intolerant. It made them a controversial and sometimes persecuted body. In this they depended on the police to defend their freedom and attend to their security, as the administrative minutes to committees and the reports of events in journals make clear.[27] This reliance on the law was linked to a strong sense of the almost sacred status of America as a righteous nation. While this was at first distinguished from the party political powers of the Washington government, it was rooted in the pioneer expectations of a land where the opportunity for personal sovereignty was protected by the constitution and the flag. The increasing dependence on the law of the land was accompanied by a sense of obligation to support the violent defense of the nation.

With its initial institutionalization, the movement still attempted to maintain its original pacifist stance such as in the proscription against war handed down by the General Assembly of the Church of God.[28] But this was soon adjusted to fit the military alignments of contemporary Western politics. By the time America entered the First World

27. Ibid., 236–7.
28. Ibid., 248.

War in April 1917, the proscription against war had been called into question. It disappeared from the minutes of the Church of God in 1921, reappeared in modified form in 1928, and disappeared for good in 1945.[29] Overall the public accommodation to contemporary racism, the reliance on law enforcement, and the increasing veneration of America as a special nation, tended to propel the Pentecostal movement along the pathway of subsumed transcendence once again. It is hardly surprising that this also left them vulnerable to the nation state's dependence on money.

As Wacker points out, the pragmatism of the emerging Pentecostal movement was directly connected to the "classically American sentiment"[30] of the pursuit of autonomy, manifest in the generally individualistic entrepreneurial approach to work.[31] The research of André Droogers on the later charismatics similarly recognizes the influence of individualism.[32] There appear to have been two particular points of vulnerability. Firstly, the practice of living by faith, while counterpolitical at root, carried a propensity for accommodation to other people and cultures. Karla Poewe shows how this cultural openness, although partly responsible for the capacity of the new transcendence to overwhelm biopower with love, as we shall shortly consider, was also vulnerable to the cultural mainstream and its orientation to the individual pursuit of financial gain. Secondly, the practice of faith all too easily became a covert, at best unconscious, at worst conscious, means of accumulating wealth. In this context, church life, ministry, and mission could all too easily become deeply parasitic on capitalism.

29. Ibid., 248.

30. Ibid., 29.

31. Ibid., 213–16.

32. Droogers, "The Normalization of Religious Experience," 34.

(C) REDISCOVERING A THEOLOGY OF THE HOLY SPIRIT

The partial colonization of the Pentecostal-Charismatic movement by sovereignty recollects the increasingly familiar process of revelation and fall paralleled in the history of both Israel and the church. Now it was happening yet again in the twentieth century. The sequence of events certainly demonstrates the power of the empire system and its ability to colonize relationships, mindsets, and spiritual movements. But there is an important difference today, which as I have already suggested is of eschatological proportions. That is to say we are at another fullness of times, but this time the partnership of church and empire is culminating in an eschatological overreach that has the capacity for the emergence of what the apostle Paul refers to as a new humanity.[33] All that is lacking is a transforming expectation of the nature of the transcendence that is once more present. Or to put it another way, there is an absence of a fully applied incarnational theology of the Holy Spirit as the Spirit of Jesus. This sense of something seriously missing in the understanding of the way the Holy Spirit operates, or what the theologians call pneumatology, has been frequently expressed over the last few decades. The Finnish theologian Veli-Matti Kärkkäinen refers to it as a "deficit of the Holy Spirit"[34] and as Rowan Williams puts it, "Many writers have remarked a certain poverty in theological reflection on the Holy Spirit in Western Christianity over the last decades."[35]

---

33. Eph 2:15; 4:13.

34. Kärkkäinen, *Pneumatology*, 17.

35. Williams, *On Christian Theology*, 107.

(1) The Spirit of Jesus

Beginning with the testimony of Jesus in the gospel narratives, we can say that the role of the Holy Spirit after the incarnation is to remind the church of the life and teaching of Jesus and its culmination in his death and resurrection. Just as it is necessary to argue from Jesus to God in order to arrive at a truly incarnational understanding of God the Father, in the same way it is necessary to argue from Jesus to the Holy Spirit. As John's gospel has it, "the Helper, the Holy Spirit, whom the Father will send in My name, He will teach you all things, and bring to your remembrance all that I said to you."[36] At the heart of these "all things" were Jesus' statements about his identification with the Father and the contrast between the loving rule of God and the imperial politics of Rome.

Given that the Holy Spirit poured out in the Pentecostal visitations of the last century is the Spirit of Jesus, then we can expect that the whole incarnational lifestyle of Jesus in the midst of the empire system is also the politics of the Spirit. So, taking as our example three incidents of the essentially revolutionary stance that Jesus took towards the temple powers, we can expect to find there the Spirit's attitude towards the contemporary Western system that is in part their descendant. As contemporary research shows, the temple in the gospel narratives was by no means simply the religious center of first-century Jewish life. It was also the locus of law and commerce. Even more significantly, the high-priestly family of Annas and Caiaphas was the puppet representative of Roman power in the south of Israel, just as Herod was in the north.[37] What happened in the temple implicated not just the Jewish authorities but the power

36. John 14:26.
37. Horsley, *Jesus and Empire*, 34.

of Rome behind them. The first of these incidents in the temple is Luke's account of the adolescent Jesus beginning to set out his distinctive stance from that of both his parents and the Jewish authorities. It clearly involved significantly countercultural behavior towards the Jewish teachers, and apparent disobedience to his mother and father. When it was over, Luke points out that Jesus then submitted to his parents. But it was now a submission signaling a distinctly countercultural direction. His transcendent father's business was not primarily his human father's business, and his theology was not the normative doctrine of the contemporary teachers.[38] Secondly, John's account of Jesus' demonstration in the temple at the commencement of his public ministry specifically records his attack on the already strong alignment of the sacrifice system with monetary exchange.[39] Thirdly, the synoptic account of a second demonstration in the temple at the end of Jesus' ministry compares Israel's original covenant of blessing for the nations with a violent economics of empire characterized as robbery.[40] At both the beginning and the end of this sequence, the public challenge to the status quo was followed by a period of what can be called radical submission. Radical, because it proceeded in the aftershock of Jesus' clear positioning of himself counter to the established authorities; submission, because rather than establishing himself in an alternative sovereignty he responds to their reactions in a loving spirit. This political rhythm of radical subversion and radical submission can be seen repeated in the Acts of the apostles and to some extent in the early church fathers. With the partnership of church and empire from the fourth century onwards, it disappeared almost completely from the main-

38. Luke 2:42–52.

39. John 2:13–16.

40. Mark 11:15–18.

stream life of the church, appearing, from time to time, as chapter 3 has indicated, in the history of the love stream.

In the course of my research I found myself asking what the Holy Spirit might have been doing when so often displaced from the mainstream life of the church. It seems to me that, like Jesus, he would have been identifying with the poor and oppressed and those relegated to the margins of the social mainstream. So rather than attempting a theology of the Holy Spirit in what is deliberately a brief book, it is the intention here simply to look at signs of the Spirit at work in distinctly incarnational ways at the margins of Western society in the period leading up to the advent of the Pentecostal-Charismatic movement. From these preparatory developments it will then be possible to indicate the direction that the fullness of the Spirit can be expected to take. Two particularly significant antecedents are the nineteenth-century civil disobedience associated with Oberlin College, described by Donald Dayton in his book *Discovering an Evangelical Heritage*, and the cultural accommodation practiced by the faith missions, explored by Karla Poewe in *Charismatic Christianity as Global Culture*.

(2) The Holy Spirit and civil disobedience

Like the characters described in the previous chapter, those who continued to translate the "love stream" into daily life were listening to the Holy Spirit teaching them new things. This was despite the increasing deficit of understanding and displacement of the Spirit's presence from the form and doctrine of Christian life. We have already seen how William Penn made his way to the New World of North America, a journey similarly undertaken by many radical followers of Jesus whose challenge to the status quo of Western European Christendom had brought them into conflict with the authorities of church and state. In the end, as we shall see, the acclaimed constitution that came into place to undergird the New World failed to safeguard it from the deep structural assumptions of the old Christendom paradigm. But while their successors generally yielded to the same process of pragmatic adaptation to sovereignty that we have observed in the centuries before and after them, it is likely that it was the seed of their lives that made North America such fertile ground for the Pentecostal-Charismatic outpourings.

The biggest sign of the underlying imperial paradigm was the acceptance of slavery as a norm in the commercial development of the New World. Dayton's research has particularly drawn attention to the tradition of civil disobedience that arose in the mid nineteenth century to challenge this. He draws special attention to the example of the students and faculty of Oberlin College during the presidency of Charles Finney. Finney's theology of atonement strongly rejected the idea of the appeasement of an offended sovereign God, and his consequent view of the cross as the ultimate reach of God's incarnation clearly positioned the kingdom of God as a template for socio-political reform. We have seen how normative the alignment of the church with the status quo had become. It followed that anything the Spirit of Jesus taught that was contrary to this was bound to be very difficult to receive and that teachings of Jesus or the apostles that seemed to vouchsafe the status quo had been strongly emphasized for many centuries. Hence Jesus' advice to "render to Caesar the things that are Caesar's," and Peter's and Paul's similar encouragements to submit to "the powers that be"[41] were applied without taking into account the radical acts of subversion that preceded them.[42]

41. Mark 12:17; 1 Pet 2:13–15; Rom 13:1–5.
42. Mark 11:15–17; Acts 4:18–20; Acts 23:1–5.

The result of all this was that the order of the day seemed irresistible and it became almost impossible to reimagine a genuinely egalitarian holy politics. Dayton describes in detail how this difficulty was overcome at Oberlin College. Here a concept of a higher law than the state was developed in opposition to the Fugitive Slave Law of 1850, in the context of the support and rescue of fugitive slaves.[43] In this situation, Henry E. Peck, associate professor of mental and moral philosophy at Oberlin, clearly recognized civil disobedience to be a necessary part of Christian discipleship. As he put it: "We must obey God always, and human law, social and civil, when we can. . . . This Divine Will was well expounded in the life of Christ . . . those who follow Him, should minister to the poor and needy; that the poor and forlorn would be blessed by it; that those 'sick and in prison' would be cheered by it; and that it would strike the iron from countless wretches unjustly bound."[44] Students and faculty engaged in civil disobedience, not only by harboring and hiding fugitive slaves, but in some cases invading the South to free them. Members of the college served prison sentences of four years, five years, and twelve years for such activities. It all came to a head in the "Oberlin-Wellington Rescue Case" in the summer of 1858 when armed men from the South recaptured John Price, a fugitive slave being harbored at Oberlin. While they were holding him at a hotel in nearby Wellington, students and faculty stormed the hotel, rescued him, and hid him in the home of Professor J. H. Fairchild, who became Finney's successor.[45]

At first sight it is hard to imagine how a republican nation state like the United States, whose constitution

43. Dayton, *Discovering an Evangelical Heritage*, 49–50.

44. Ibid., 49.

45. Ibid., 48.

purposes "to establish Justice, insure domestic Tranquility, provide for the common defence, promote the general Welfare, and secure the Blessings of Liberty to ourselves and our Posterity," could pass a law supporting slavery. This is especially so given that those fleeing to the New World were attempting to escape those aspects of the unrestrained authority of empire of which slavery was one. However, although the new state, and indeed the whole Western nation state project,[46] was intended to separate the powers of church and state to prevent them dominating each other to the detriment of the peace, the underlying status quo of sovereign power continued. The separation of the powers was only superficial, and the foundational role of sovereignty remained in place.

Both Jurgen Habermas and Agamben have helpfully explained how this continued to be the case in both constitutional monarchies and republics. Habermas shows that with the shift from royal to popular sovereignty, the rights of subjects were transformed into human and civil rights. Although ideally and in principle this seemed to guarantee political autonomy to everyone, it only worked in the context of what he terms the *Volksgeist*, a unique corporate spirit of the people that could only have arisen from the consciousness of a people defined by subjection to state power. In this way rights were predicated on a primary conscious acquiescence to the idea of sovereign power. The sovereignty of the people was thereby mediated through the political structures of the city or nation state.[47] The depths of this perception are underlined by the ambiguous semantics of the Latin word *populus* that has been carried over into the European languages and carries both the referent

46. See chapter two.

47. Habermas, "The European Nation-State: On the Past and Future of Sovereignty and Citizenship," 404.

81

of people as the general population and the People as a corporate identity. As we saw in chapter 3, Agamben notes how this tends to reinforce the subjugation of the people as the excluded multitude, by the People as sovereign power.[48] So even in the case of the American Constitution, which seems to vouchsafe freedom, the rule of sovereignty as the system for peace was never called into question. In this way the particular political character of the gospel was undermined. In order for the essentially loving, egalitarian nature of divine-human relationships to be resumed, the authority of state law has to be relativized by a proper understanding of the holy political role of civil disobedience.

(2) Living by faith and naked life

Once the Holy Spirit is recognized as the carrier of a different kind of power to sovereignty, the possibility of understanding and participating in that alternative power becomes real. This alternative power, or kenarchy, substantiates peace through love by an exercise of faith. Faith in this context is neither otherworldly nor theoretical, but intensely practical in the way it works. Karla Poewe's research suggests that the exercise of living by faith, or what she also calls "faith prayer,"[49] is one of the primary roots of the Pentecostal outpourings. She identifies this kind of faith with the empathy with the "other" expressed in the nineteenth-century faith missions. She explains this in terms of a total abandonment to God and his image in other humans of an alien culture that culminated in the wholehearted embrace of the indigenous host community. She cites the founding tenets of the China Inland Mission as classic examples in

48. Agamben, *Means Without End. Notes on Politics*, 28–34.
49. Poewe (ed.), *Charismatic Christianity as Global Culture*, 10.

which the adoption of Chinese dress and lifestyle was a requirement for missionary work.[50] Viewed in this way, living by faith is an inclusive, loving accommodation to God and other people, based on surrender and receptivity. As Poewe explains, it directly challenges the modern Western mindset. The result is a reversal of "the centrality of the rational, of calculated doing, of articulate verbal skills, of doctrine, and of things Western."[51] This process of faith moves from the non-rational to the rational, from happening to doing, from experience to talk, from sign to meaning, and from spiritual gifts to social engagement. Faith embraces a relational encounter, based on love not sovereign power, and the proceeding story moves from relationship to action and from demonstration to theology.

Poewe emphasizes the impact of this operation of faith in relation to financial and material provision in a way that provides important insight into the economics of Pentecostal-Charismatic primitivism. Their total dependence on God had the effect of dislodging their dependence on the rational economics of twentieth-century capitalism and basing their hope for practical provision on a love-motivated alignment with the material world as displayed in the narratives of the incarnation. As Matthew's gospel describes Jesus' advice:

> "Do not worry then, saying, 'What will we eat?' or 'What will we drink?' or 'What will we wear for clothing?' For the Gentiles eagerly seek all these things; for your heavenly Father knows that you need all these things. But seek first His

50. Grubb, *C. T. Studd, Cricketer and Pioneer*, 54.

51. Poewe, "The Nature, Globality and History of Charismatic Christianity," 12.

> kingdom and His righteousness, and all these things will be added to you."[52]

We have already seen the vulnerability of the Pentecostal-Charismatic movement to the burgeoning commodification of twentieth-century biopower. Poewe's analysis discloses instead the practical eschatological potential of living by faith. For the same attitude that renders Pentecostal-Charismatic primitivism vulnerable to biopower, can, if aligned with the radical incarnational dynamic of the Spirit of Jesus, meet the experience of naked life with a transformative resource able to subvert biopower with love. Perceiving that we are all captive to the control exercised by the commodification of everything, Pentecostal-Charismatics can also recognize that the baptism of the Spirit carries the possibility, even the necessity, of breaking free from biopower. Once we are ready to take appropriate action to subvert the status quo by civil disobedience when necessary, then biopower loses its controlling claim to the totality of human life. Instead we are free to reimagine a love-motivated world. By practicing an accommodating, inclusive, loving attitude of faith together with those emerging with us as its victims across the whole surface of the Western system, we can lay hold of the means to change it. In this context it is important to realize that the Holy Spirit is alongside all of us, whether orientated to a sacred or secular perspective, not only because the Spirit is "poured out on all flesh"[53] but especially because a God who is like Jesus must certainly have come with the church into this devastating partnership with empire, just like they came with the Jews into theirs.

---

52. Matt 6:31–33.

53. Acts 2:17.

In conclusion, bringing together these two crucial characteristics of the Holy Spirit's working, we can say with some confidence that a radical subversion-submission process, lived by faith, is able to join with the naked life of the multitude that is the inevitable overkill of biopower and achieve the shift from sovereignty to kenarchy. The interminable transformations of the church-empire partnership can at last give way to the incarnational rhythm of revolutionary activism and life-laying-down submissive love.

5

Myths and Obstacles

THIS FINAL CHAPTER AIMS to clear away some of the most resistant obstacles to the mindset change from sovereignty to love. In the light of the experiences of my own journey and interaction with others on a similar path, the foremost of these are likely to be deep within the identity of the individuals attempting this change. The abandonment to the other that characterizes living by faith is, after all, no easy choice to make. But love is not only the motivation for subverting biopower, it is also the very means to the radical submission to the other that continues to embed kenarchy in and through the whole of personal and corporate life. We will return to this lifelong collaboration in radical transcendence in the final section of the chapter. But in order to reach such a naked kenarchy it is necessary to identify some of the most deeply held theopolitical myths and obstacles that stand in our way. The most resilient of these can be summed up in three categories, the first of which consists of problematic beliefs about the gospel narratives or "gospel myths" that significantly undermine the Jesus story. The second is made up of idolatrous perspectives towards Britain, the United States of America, and particularly Israel that regard all three nation states as in some sense "promised lands." Finally come the peculiar beliefs about the end times derived from thinking consequent on the fall of the church that I term "ghastly eschatologies."

(A) GOSPEL MYTHS

There are two persistent and quite dogmatic attitudes to the gospel narratives that either relegate them to the category of unreliable myth or perpetuate new myths about them. The first of these stems from rationalistic skepticism about the historical reliability of the gospel testimony, and the second from a conservative evangelical insistence on submitting that testimony to the Bible as a whole. In their different ways, both of these attitudes prove to be obstacles to the kind of approach to the Jesus story advocated in this book. As a result they hinder the innovatory access to radical transcendence set out at the end of the previous chapter.

(1) Doubts about the historical Jesus

Beginning with the skeptical rationalist's doubt about the reliability of the gospels, we encounter the typical claim that we can know little for certain about the historical Jesus. As it turns out, what remains of the person of Jesus after the skeptic has finished her or his assessment of the evidence, is often quite supportive of the general view of the gospels. Donald Cupitt, for example, is pretty clear that the "not quite unreachable figure of Jesus" was morally opposed to Roman sovereignty.[1] But nevertheless the overall effect of the rationalists' perspective is to undermine the ground for

1. Cupitt, "The Christ of Christendom," 145.

faith in the testimony of Jesus. The skeptical critic generally cites the conclusions of form and textual criticism as the source of their doubt. Form or redaction criticism searches out and purports to discover earlier written and oral traditions beneath the surface of the gospel text, while textual criticism investigates differences in the actual text of the various narratives. It is not my intention here to explore or rebut the extensive theoretical work of either type of scholarship. There is nothing necessarily undermining of the gospel testimony in such approaches to the text, and historical and textual criticism can shed real light on the gospel narratives. But the problem with such theories is that they often conceal a rationalistic rejection of significant parts of the gospel accounts simply because of the miraculous claims that they contain. It is my contention that it is the rational rejection of the transcendent because of its supposed essential alignment with domination and oppression consequent on its subsumption by sovereignty that lies behind this. Whether it is Rudolph Bultmann's opinion that modern men "take it for granted that the course of nature and history . . . is nowhere interrupted by the intervention of supernatural powers"[2] or John Caputo's more recent objection to miracles as "rouged spectacular presence" and "profane magic,"[3] the real problem appears to be with the transcendent nature of the story, not the historical reliability of the text. For the modern rationalist, transcendent claims are irrational by definition. This position has particular influence on the arguments for the dating of the gospels where prophecies related to the fall of Jerusalem are used as reasons for a late date on the assumption that they must have been written after the event and could not be

2. Bultmann, *Jesus Christ and Mythology*, 16.
3. Caputo, *The Weakness of God*, 40, 42, 44.

actual prophecies.[4] To summarize, skepticism towards the New Testament narratives tends to involve an inflated view of the rational judgment of the modern mind that superimposes a kind of secular superiority where human reason retakes the level of supreme authority previously held by religious institutions.

(2) The Biblicists' Jesus

The particular conservative evangelical position that I am identifying as a second category of gospel myth insists on submitting the gospel testimony to an already existing theology of God. But this theology has in fact been developed through the discernment and application of a systematic scheme from the Bible as a whole, that is then used to interpret the gospel testimony to Jesus rather than the other way round. The Jesus we thereby end up with is a mythical and often contradictory one, emerging from a diverse amalgam of perspectives on the divine. This approach to the gospel testimony is based on what is actually a Biblicist rather than a Christian view of the Scriptures. It is quite distinct from a fully incarnational view that makes the time, location, and content of the gospels of central importance to our understanding of the rest of the Scriptures. The problem with the Biblicist approach, as we have already seen to such devastating effect in the case of Eusebius of Caesarea, is that it is vulnerable to importing subsumed views of God and reading them into the Scriptures. If, as we have suggested in chapter 3, the Scriptures already depict the story of the embrace of ideas about God and government by the Old Testament people of God that the incarnation was intended to bring to a complete end, then this is highly problematic.

4. Guthrie, *New Testament Introduction*, 43.

It means that the conservative evangelical approach to the Bible seriously mythologizes the character and purpose of the incarnation.

This is not at all to say that the incarnation can be divorced from the rest of Scripture; far from it. It is clearly pointed towards within the Old Testament and expanded through the rest of the New Testament writings. On their own testimony the gospels claim to fulfill the Old Testament law and prophets and promise the Holy Spirit as the means to vouchsafe the incarnation story into the future. But it is also clear from the gospels themselves that the intention of the revelation of God in Jesus is to reinterpret the rest of the Scriptures in its light and not to subject the Jesus story to the law and the prophets. In this connection Giorgio Agamben has helpfully drawn attention to Paul's ambivalent use of the Greek word *katargēsis*, often translated as "abolish."[5] It is a word that can help us grapple with the way that Jesus brought to an end the partially subsumed perception of God's governance in the Old Testament. The word *katargēsis* conveys both the fullness and final end of a matter. As chapter 3 has already indicated, Jesus fulfilled and consummated the Old Testament understanding of law, monarchy, and temple by turning them completely upside down and inside out. Now love supersedes law, humility empties out monarchy, and the temple is his body positioned in and through the whole creation. This is difficult to grasp until one sees God and the world through the lens of the incarnation. The story of the disciples' resurrection encounter on the road to Emmaus is informative here. As Luke puts it, "we were hoping that it was He who was going to redeem Israel"[6] and it was, but not in empire terms. It was only after they had understood who Jesus was

5. 1 Cor 1:28; Agamben, *The Time That Remains*, 104–8.
6. Luke 24:21.

that "beginning with Moses and with all the prophets, He explained to them the things concerning Himself in all the Scriptures."[7]

These two perspectives, the skeptical rational and the conservative evangelical, are not so very different at root, as both are based in a positivistic approach to truth. Or to put it another way, they assume truth to be an absolute certainty to which people can be required to submit. The first, as I have already argued, has its roots in a rationalistic rejection of transcendence of the kind we have already considered at some length in chapter 1. The other originates in an equally modernistic reaction to that rejection that tries to give the Bible the same objective, rational certainty as the positivistic truth of enlightenment thinking. However, both continue to undergird the authority of sovereign power, the one without recourse to sovereign transcendence and the other with it.

What we have been talking about is what academics call "hermeneutics." This word refers to the way we make sense of something, generally a piece of writing or passage of Scripture, although it can be applied more widely, including to life itself. From the perspective being put forward here, the incarnation story of the gospels is presented as the core hermeneutic to be applied not just to understanding the rest of Scripture, but the whole of life. Two contemporary thinkers, N. T. Wright and Graham Ward, provide some helpful insight into how this operates. Coming from perspectives broadly allied to the more conservative evangelical and rational skeptic stances respectively, they nonetheless represent strongly incarnational approaches to the gospel story. Both thinkers are serious theologians, to whose theoretical work justice cannot be done here. Suffice it to say that Wright's "critical realism" view is based on a

7. Luke 24:27.

helpfully balanced recognition of the historically objective quality of the gospel material and the postmodern perception of the more subjective quality of knowledge.[8] It can be usefully synchronized with Ward's "economy of response," a practical and affective approach that intentionally engages the personal, emotional aspects of the story and is deliberately orientated to its relational rather than cerebral content.[9] By this means, adequate rational grounds for faith can be brought together with a relational encounter with the egalitarian transcendence of the incarnation.

(B) PROMISED LANDS

The second category of obstacle to the move from sovereignty to kenarchy represents a problem that is particularly deeply rooted in Britain and the United States of America. This is the manifestation of the partnership of church and empire that is religious patriotism. I am not referring here to love of one's country, but the idea that one particular country or another is especially favored by God in being positioned over against others in a morally or culturally superior manner. It tends to carry with it the idea of a special relationship or covenant with God that apparently guaranteed the nation's past and present prosperity. The thinking is that such an advantage will continue into the future as long as the nation involved keeps to certain conditions at the heart of its political construct, such as the ten commandments. While this reading of the relationship between God and nations might conceivably be defended from the Old Testament story of Israel, just as long as one avoids crucial parts of the message of the prophets, it runs counter to

---

8. Wright, *The New Testament and the People of God*, 32–36, 64.
9. Ward, *Christ and Culture*, 59.

the fullness of the divine character and purpose revealed in the incarnation. As we have already seen from Jesus' final public remonstration with the temple authorities, it was precisely this selfish promotion of national dominance that aligned Israel with empire and lost its calling to the nations.

(1) The purpose of Israel

If as God's initial promise to Abraham stated, the blessing of God is for all the families of the earth,[10] then the gift of land, culture, and people is to be stewarded for the rest of humanity. The advent of Jesus and his identification with those displaced by empire, such as women, the homeless, the asylum seeker, and the poor, made clear that the kind of society that sided with empire for its own survival and prosperity was far from the kingdom of God. Israel's chronic inability to understand their kenotic purpose as God's loving agents provided the background to the incarnation story. As chapter 2 has already pointed out, the radical prophetic stream constantly called them back to their original destiny. They were to be the means of making "wars to cease,"[11] of speaking "peace to the nations,"[12] of leveling social stratification,[13] and of bringing "justice to the nations"[14] until "the earth will be filled with the knowledge of the glory of God as the waters cover the sea."[15] As Luke's famous Magnificat sums it up in Mary's own prophecy of the incarnation, it was to pull down the mighty from their

10. Gen 12:3.
11. Ps 46:9.
12. Zech 9:10.
13. Isa 11:6.
14. Isa 42:1.
15. Hab 2:14.

thrones and exalt the lowly.[16] In these terms the purpose of Jerusalem was as the mountain of the house of the Lord to which the nations came to see the governance of God demonstrated.[17] It is this that Jesus speaks of rebuilding in three days[18] and Paul describes in Galatians as "the Jerusalem above."[19] It was this destiny that the gospel testimony saw as completed in Jesus, including the fullness of the battle prophecies of Zechariah, Jesus' most quoted Old Testament book. At the cross all the prophesied eschatological battles reached their culmination. Now "all the tribes of the earth" could "look on Me whom they have pierced . . . and . . . mourn," and not only the tribes of Israel who represented them.[20] We can say confidently from the testimony of Jesus that if there is any ongoing prophetic destiny for the Jerusalem "below" it must be as a place of inclusive blessing for all nations, including its enemies.

Despite this incarnational fulfillment in Jesus, the idea that God's covenant guarantees the ownership and rulership of the land by a particular state or people has continued to define world politics. As we have already seen, the assumption that this was the nature and purpose of God's blessing to Israel played a key part in the foundation of the Western nation state in Britain during the seventeenth century, and often continues to uphold it. Gilbert Burnet drew on the supposed sign and parallel of ancient Israel[21] in his legitimation of William and Mary, and William Paterson did the same in securing the Bank of England's currency of debt on the future prosperity of Britain. Even William

16. Cf. Luke 1:52.

17. Isa 2; Mic 4.

18. Matt 26:61; John 2:19.

19. Gal 4:26.

20. Zech 12:10; John 19:37.

21. Mitchell, *Church, Gospel, & Empire*, 123, 121.

Penn drew on an idealized view of native English justice to undergird his Holy Experiment instead of drawing on the egalitarian loving justice of the incarnation.[22] Had he done the latter he might have written kenotic love deeper into his initial configuration of the American Constitution.

(2) Subconscious mythologies of the nation state

It is this background to the Western nation state that makes patriotic practices such as the pledge of allegiance to the American flag and the singing of jingoistic national anthems, something much more than love for the land of one's adoption or birth. Personal identification with the deep subconscious mythologies of the nation state works strongly against the necessary challenge to the status quo brought about by the practice of civil disobedience advocated in the previous chapter. Romanticized notions of nationhood such as those summed up in Shakespeare's "this sceptred isle"[23] and songs like "Rule Britannia," "Land of Hope and Glory," "America the Beautiful," and "The Battle Hymn of the Republic" all occupy the space that Jesus obtained for egalitarian grace. Gratitude for the gift of a land and culture to steward for the blessing of the other nations of the world is undoubtedly a good thing, but the proud, violent national idolatry that emerges from below the surface of our supposed promised lands is dangerous and destructive.

Since the establishment of the nation state of Israel after the horrors of the Holocaust, the danger of it coming to embody the idea of God's commitment to special lands and people has been very real. Instead of encouraging Israel to pursue its ancient heritage of being a blessing

22. Murphy, *The Political Writings of William Penn,* 394.
23. Shakespeare, *King Richard II.* Act 2 scene 1.

to all the families of the earth, there has been a tendency for the United States, Britain, and other nations to invest the modern nation state of Israel with special status as a talisman of justice and blessing. Supported by American and British vetoes at the UN council, defended by atomic weapons, and financed by Western investment, it has become the archetypical symbol of the political currencies of law, violence, and money that undergird the whole Western imperial project. It is crucially important to point out here that while the parallel promotion of the Palestinian people as a rightful alternative claimant for ownership of the so-called promised land is fully understandable in the circumstances, it only replaces one symbol of sovereignty with another. In so doing it makes the more striking the destructive implications of the exclusive ownership of land for a particular people instead of its stewardship by all its inhabitants for the common good. From both a creational and incarnational perspective, land is the context for every tribe and tongue and nation to live together in peace and harmony. The current Middle Eastern tragedy is a clarion call for kenarchy coming from the very place of its source.

(C) GHASTLY ESCHATOLOGIES

Nations like Britain and the United States mistook the results of Israel's fall from stewardship into an exclusive ownership of the land as the original purpose of God. In much the same way the Evangelical and Pentecostal-Charismatic churches have tended to take on a similar view of the church. They have regarded God's new covenant as the evidence that the church are God's specially protected favorites on planet earth, rather than the agents of grace for the poor, strangers, and enemies. For this reason the misapplication of God's covenant with the land of Israel often continues to feature in the church's expectations for the future.

(1) Dispensational eschatologies

This privileged position for the church is particularly characteristic of the modern dispensational eschatologies that center round the church's future relationship to an anticipated thousand years of peace. These are the amillennial, premillennial, and postmillennial theories that have occupied much theological debate about the end times. It is especially true of the premillennial eschatologies that posit the removal of the church prior to a supposed great tribulation that befalls the rest of humanity before the establishment of a millennial reign of peace centered on a reconstituted Israel complete with Jerusalem and its temple. These theories came to great public prominence in the 1970s through Hal Lindsey's *The Late Great Planet Earth* and more recently the *Left Behind* series of books and films from Tim LaHaye and Jerry B. Jenkins. What is distinctive and particularly problematic about these various eschatologies is the assumption that the climax to the salvation story is a new and cosmic Christian empire with Jesus on the throne and the neo-nations of Israel and the church as his ruling cadres.

The basic problem with these dispensational eschatologies is that they reintroduce the imperial view of God that Jesus came to fulfill and correct. This is by no means a merely esoteric matter of interesting theological speculations on the nature of the end times. These are life and death issues that need to be faced. It is well documented that President George Bush Junior's policy on the Middle East was directly influenced by such eschatologies.[24] The

24. See, for example, Yaakov Ariel, "Messianic Hopes and Middle East Politics: the Influence of Millennial Faith on American

highly influential worldwide intercessory movement has been at least partly infected by them. In this way they have inadvertently been a means of exacerbating some of the very problems they had intended to overcome and have continued the colonization of the Pentecostal-Charismatic movement by biopower in ways considered in the previous chapter.

It is not primarily the specifics of an eschatology that make it ghastly, although for sure some details are quite dreadful, but the theological and political assumptions that drive it. A properly incarnational theology always argues from Jesus to God. This works forwards as well as backwards. That is to say that our expectations about the future peace that Jesus came to bring needs to be of the same substance as the incarnation. Any second coming of the gospel Jesus will manifest the same essential kenotic lordship as the first coming. So we can say that concepts of future victory for the church and judgment on its enemies that run counter to Jesus' demonstrations of victory and treatment of his enemies cannot belong to the future kingdom of God. This means that a Jesus hermeneutic has to be applied to the epistles as well as the Old Testament and particularly the Revelation. The latter clearly stands together with the few brief passages of Jesus' own apocalyptic in the counterpolitical stream of the Old Testament prophets. Seen this way the Revelation and Jesus' apocalyptic are about exposing the here and now of the status quo, more than providing precise details of an as yet unknown future. Once this is understood the Revelation becomes an extraordinarily practical handbook for the radical activism of subversion-submission spelt out in the previous chapter. Martin Scott has helpfully demonstrated this in his exposition of the letters to the seven churches in the first three

Middle East Policies."

chapters of Revelation. He applies the message and imagery of the letters to particular city types in order to see how a city and its hinterland might best be developed for the blessing of the nations.[25] In their book *Unveiling Empire*[26] Wes Howard-Brook and Anthony Gwyther give a comprehensive overview of what a radical political interpretation of the apocalypse might look like when applied to an imperial society in any generation.

Donald Dayton has done comprehensive work on the rise of the premillennial eschatological theories we have been considering here.[27] He helpfully explores their roots in the tension between the dispensational eschatological views of John Wesley's eighteenth-century associate John Fletcher and Wesley's much more this-worldly reformist and incarnational approach. He explores how the futuristic premillennial views came to dominate a century later, particularly as developed in the writings of the Plymouth Brethren evangelist J. N. Darby. Dayton explains this in terms of a deep frustration with the perceived failure of the evangelical justice agenda such as that characterized by Oberlin College despite the fact that, as we have seen already, he regards that movement as itself a primary harbinger of the Pentecostal-Charismatic outpourings. This shows how easily the church becomes vulnerable to a crisis of faith when egalitarian grace fails to be properly earthed and the expected rule of peace seems to be delayed. This is both challenging and encouraging. Challenging, because it shows how the failure to have a properly incarnational perspective reduces the gospel to the expectation that it is merely about immediate breakthrough for personal bless-

25. Scott, *Impacting the City*.

26. Howard-Brook and Gwyther, *Unveiling Empire: Reading Revelation Then and Now*.

27. See Dayton, "The Rise of Premillennialism," 145.

ing. It exposes a truncated gospel that assumes that either we get permanently healed or socially freed in the present or we simply wait for our sufferings to be justified sometime in the future. Encouraging, because, notwithstanding the apparent crisis of faith that led to the rise of such ghastly eschatologies, the utter abandonment to God of the late-nineteenth-century people of faith, despite their vulnerability to empire, led to an unprecedented outpouring of transcendent grace.

(2) The future hope of the neo-Marxists

It is this tendency to carry or reintroduce sovereign power into future configurations of ultimate peace, despite an originally egalitarian agenda, that aligns these Christian eschatologies with the future hope of the neo-Marxists. This is not as unlikely a connection as it may at first appear, for it turns out that they too are in danger of configuring a future hope that brings with it the same disease that their diagnosis set out to remedy. For while Hardt and Negri, as we have seen, regard Judeo-Christian love as a political act that constructs the multitude,[28] the eschatological future of that multitude transpires to be for it "to express itself autonomously and rule itself."[29] Negri describes this as an individuated autonomy guaranteed by an "absolute democracy."[30] Admittedly he distinguishes between the absolutism of democracy and the absolutism of sovereignty, which he regards as totalitarian. But the specter of a multitude of individuals safeguarding one another's autonomy by democratic process is only sovereignty by another name. In

28. Hardt and Negri, *Multitude*, 352.

29. Ibid., 101.

30. Negri, *Insurgencies*, 12.

the genealogy of the multiplication of sovereign power from totalitarianism, it is clear that autonomy is the final indivisible expression of personal sovereignty. The neo-Marxists rightfully disassociate themselves from the injustices of the sovereignty of the People over the multitude such as seen in the former Soviet Union. However, they still seem to anticipate a democracy that sustains the indivisible sovereign right of autonomous individuals ruling over what gifts and materials they have at their personal disposal. In the end both these transcendent and immanent eschatologies are rooted in the same misconception that sovereign power is the means to peace.

This issue of individual autonomy brings us to the crux of the matter. Love and sovereignty, love and autonomy, do not mix. Autonomy and sovereignty make the individual or corporate exercise of power the beginning point of human fulfillment. They exist in what the philosophers call a subalternate relationship. That is to say there can be sovereignty without autonomy, but not autonomy without sovereignty. Autonomy is the individual form of sovereign power. Kenarchy, however, begins with love. Love is about self-giving mutual service. It begins by recognizing oneself as a love gift in relationship to another. If it is the case that this love gift originates with and emanates from the divine, then this takes love to an even deeper corporate dimension. Seen in this way, intimacy with the divine is the resource that complements the potential power of naked life and releases the gifts of God and humanity to equip a new humanity to live in the fullness of self-giving love and mutual service. From the neo-Marxist perspective this appears weak and acquiescent to the oppressive, toxic forms of subsumed transcendence that it rightly regards as having abused submission, service, and sacrifice to maintain oppressive regimes. In this they remain provisionally aligned with the functional rejection of transcendence of the modern rationalists. But as we have seen, the desire to break out of the contemporary fullness of biopower has nevertheless brought them to return to the resource of Judeo-Christian love.

So although the full implications of this move are masked by their intense suspicion of transcendence, the challenge that Judeo-Christian love presents to autonomy needs to be exposed. For the kind of Christian love that complements the Jewish tradition is more than an initial motivation to action, it is the very substance of egalitarian politics. The difficulty that neo-Marxists have with the implications of this are eloquently expressed by Alain Badiou in his book *In Praise of Love*, where he states, "In my opinion, the politics of love is a meaningless expression. Principally because there are people in politics one doesn't love . . . that's undeniable, nobody can expect us to love them."[31] He goes on to identify "them" as one's enemies. As he states, "The issue of the enemy is completely foreign to the question of love."[32] But the heart of kenarchy is quite the opposite of this. Here love culminates in the cross and resurrection. The cross of Jesus demonstrates a life fully given in the love and service of others. This is the utter reversal of the sacrifice of oneself for the sovereignty of one's people, country, or individual autonomy. It is the giving of oneself within the gift of God's egalitarian grace to the farthest reach of the other's position, at the utter risk of one's own life. Love cannot and will not coerce, but it encompasses the distance across which another, even one's enemies, can approach if they will. Far from meaningless, for Jesus, love is politics, and love of one's enemy is at its heart.

31. Badiou, *In Praise of Love*, 57.
32. Ibid., 59.

GIVING IN TO LOVE

Love does not only, as Hardt and Negri put it, construct the multitude. It needs to transform and sustain it. In any case it is surely impossible to love a fellow human being and not be willing to lay one's life down to change the world into a just and egalitarian place for them. But while the drive to love is at times overwhelming, it has to be acknowledged that to live out a radically subversive, radically submissive rhythm of love of the kind considered here is not easy. To keep laying one's life down in the daily choices of living can only be sustained if there is hope of resurrection. Hardt and Negri, quoting the love song of Solomon, speak of a love as strong as death.[33] Resurrection substantiates this kind of love. It is not for our own sake we need this; dying is not the issue. Jesus thought the risk worth taking, and so might we. It is not for some distant eschatological future that we need the hope of resurrection, but for the emergence of the new humanity in which it issues. This is surely why Paul says, "if Christ has not been raised . . . we are of all men most to be pitied."[34] We are, as he puts it, quoting the Psalmist, "being put to death all day long."[35] Not because he regards immanent life as without value, but precisely because it is so valuable. It is this resurrection love that moves beyond the political act that constructs the multitude and begins to transform and sustain it in equality, justice, and prosperity. It is for this reason that Ray Mayhew, drawing on N. T. Wright, describes resurrection as *the* political act.[36] This resurrection love substantiates the multitude. Laying one's

33. Hardt and Negri, *Multitude*, 352.

34. 1 Cor 15:17, 19.

35. Rom 8:36.

36. Mayhew, "Turning the Tables, Resurrection as Revolution," 1.

life down into this process of dying and rising is a huge challenge. We face the fact almost daily that it is a struggle to succeed in expressing this kind of love towards those dearest to us, let alone our enemies. The desire for autonomy, for personal sovereignty, is so deeply embedded in our identity that we fight to hold onto it. I remember from years ago the words of a young woman which resounded with such human representativeness they have stayed with me ever since. Responding with initial desire to the message of incarnation she cried out, "I love what you say; I love what you do . . . But I'm not having Jesus, I'm not having God, I'm not having anyone tell me how to live my life." Perhaps she had heard domination in the messengers of transcendence, but however purely the call of love is expressed, it discomforts personal autonomy. This is the heart of the matter. Will we give in to love? Will we subvert and submit our autonomy to life-laying-down loving relationship for the sake of the other, even our enemy? If this kind of incarnational loving transcendence is once again presenting itself to and in the contemporary fullness of biopower, then such a politics is once again possible. It has been the unwillingness of the people of God to accept such a gift that has constituted the fall of the church. The gift remains.

Bibliography

Agamben, Giorgio. *Means Without End. Notes on Politics*. Translated by Vincenzo Binetti and Cesare Casarino. Minneapolis and London: University of Minnesota Press, 2000.

———. *State of Exception*. Translated by Kevin Attell. Chicago and London: The University of Chicago Press, 2005.

———. *The Time That Remains. A Commentary on the Letter to the Romans*. Stanford, California: Stanford University Press, 2005.

Ariel, Yaakov. "Messianic Hopes and Middle East Politics: the Influence of Millennial Faith on American Middle East Policies." LISA e-journal. Vol. IX - n°1 | 2011: Religion and Politics in the English-speaking World: Historical and Contemporary Links.

Arnott, John. *The Father's Blessing*. Orlando, Florida: Creation House, 1995.

Badiou, Alain, with Nicolas Truong. *In Praise of Love*. Translated by Peter Bush. London: Serpent's Tail, 2012.

Barrett, David. "The Worldwide Holy Spirit Renewal." In *The Century of the Holy Spirit* by Vinson Synan. Nashville, Tennessee: Thomas Nelson, 2001.

Bartleman, Frank. *Azusa Street*. Plainfield, New Jersey: Logos International, 1980.

Bennett, Dennis J. *Nine O'clock in the Morning*. Plainfield, New Jersey: Logos International, 1970.

Bultmann, Rudolph. *Jesus Christ and Mythology*. London: SCM, 1958.

Caputo, John. *The Weakness of God. A Theology of the Event*. Bloomington and Indianapolis: Indiana University Press, 2006.

Carter, Warren. *Matthew and Empire*. Harrisburg: Trinity Press, 2001.

Claydon, Tony. *William III and the Godly Revolution*. Cambridge: Cambridge University Press, 1996.

Cowley, Jason. "The coming battle over land and property." *The New Statesman*, October 18, 2010.

Bibliography

Crossan, John Dominic, and Jonathan L. Reed. *In Search of Paul*. New York: HarperSanFrancisco, 2004.

Cupitt, Donald. "The Christ of Christendom." In *The Myth of God Incarnate*, edited by John Hick. London: SCM Press, 1977.

Dayton, Donald. *Discovering an Evangelical Heritage*. Grand Rapids, Michigan: Baker Academic, 2011.

———. "The Rise of Premillennialism." In *Theological Roots of Pentecostalism*. Peabody, Massachusetts: Hendrickson Publishers, 2007.

de Lubac, Henri, SJ. *Corpus Mysticum*. Translated by Gemma Simmonds, CJ. London: SCM Press, 2006.

Droogers, André. "The Normalization of Religious Experience." In *Charismatic Christianity as Global Culture*, edited by Karla Poewe. Columbia, South Carolina: University of South Carolina Press, 1994.

Eusebius of Caesarea. *The History of the Church*. Translated by G. A. Williamson. London: Penguin Books, 1965.

Fields, Darrell, with Lorrie Fields. *The Seed of a Nation*. New York: Morgan James Publishing, 2008.

Foucault, Michel. *The History of Sexuality*, vol. I. Translated by Robert Hurley. London: Penguin Books, 1990.

Grubb, Norman P. *C. T. Studd, Cricketer and Pioneer*. London: Lutterworth Press, 1965.

Guthrie, Donald. *New Testament Introduction*. London: The Tyndale Press, 1965.

Habermas, Jurgen. "The European Nation-State: On the Past and Future of Sovereignty and Citizenship." In *Public Culture*, translated by Ciaran Cronin. Durham, North Carolina: Duke University Press, 1998.

Hardt, Michael, and Antonio Negri. *Empire*. Cambridge, Massachusetts and London, England: Harvard University Press, 2000.

———. *Multitude*. New York: Penguin Books, 2004.

Hepden, Stephen. "The Impact of Racial Inclusivity in the Azusa Street Revival." MTh diss., University of Manchester, 2008.

Hocken, Peter. *The Challenges of the Pentecostal, Charismatic and Messianic Jewish Movements*. Farnham, Surrey and Burlington, Vermont: Ashgate, 2009.

Hollenweger, W. J. "The Pentecostal Elites and the Pentecostal Poor." In *Charismatic Christianity as Global Culture*, edited by Karla Poewe. Columbia, South Carolina: University of South Carolina Press, 1994.

Hollerich, M. J. *Eusebius of Caesarea's Commentary on Isaiah*. Oxford: Clarendon Press, 1999.

Horsley, Richard. *Jesus and Empire*. Minneapolis: Fortress Press, 2003.

Howard-Brook, Wesley, and Anthony Gwyther. *Unveiling Empire*. Maryknoll, New York: Orbis Books, 1999.

Jenkins, Philip. *The Next Christendom*. Oxford: Oxford University Press, 2002.

Johnson, Todd M. "The Global Dynamics of the Pentecostal and Charismatic Renewal." Published online: Springer Science + Business Media, LLC, 2009.

Kärkkäinen, Veli-Matti. *Pneumatology*. Grand Rapids, Michigan: Baker Academic, 2002.

Lake, Kirsopp. *The Epistle to Diognetus*. A pamphlet from Kessinger Publishing, extracted from *The Apostolic Fathers*. London: Heinemann, New York: Macmillan, 1912–13.

Ma, Wonsuk. "When the Poor are Fired Up." In *Transformation: An International Journal of Holistic Mission Studies*. January 2007, 24: 28–34.

Mayhew, Ray. "Turning the Tables, Resurrection as Revolution." Review of N. T. Wright, *The Resurrection of the Son of God*. No pages. Online: http://tinyurl.com/659lokn.

McIntosh, Alastair. *Soil and Soul: People versus Corporate Power*. London: Aurum Press, 2001.

Mitchell, Roger Haydon. *Church, Gospel, & Empire*. Eugene, Oregon: Wipf and Stock, 2011.

Murphy, Andrew R. *The Political Writings of William Penn*. Indianapolis: Liberty Fund, 2002.

Negri, Antonio. *Insurgencies*. Minneapolis and London: University of Minnesota Press, 2009.

Nietzsche, Friedrich. *The Gay Science*. Translated by Walter Kaufmann. New York: Vintage Books, 1974.

O'Donovan, Oliver, and Joan Lockwood O'Donovan. *From Irenaeus to Grotius*. Grand Rapids, Michigan: William B. Eerdmans Publishing Co., 1999.

Poewe, Karla, ed. *Charismatic Christianity as Global Culture*. Columbia, South Carolina: University of South Carolina Press, 1994.

Reader's Digest, The. *Oxford Complete Word Finder*. London: The Reader's Digest Association Ltd, 1993.

Robson, Michael. *St Francis of Assisi, The Legend and the Life*. Cassell, London: Geoffrey Chapman, 1997.

Bibliography

Sabatier, Paul. *Life of St Francis of Assisi*. Translated by Louise Seymour Houghton. London: Hodder and Stoughton, 1919.

Scott, Martin. *Impacting the City*. Tonbridge: Sovereign World, 2005.

Shakespeare, William. *King Richard II*. Act 2 scene 1.

Synan, Vinson. *The Century of the Holy Spirit. 100 Years of Pentecostal and Charismatic Renewal* 1901-2001. Nashville, Tennessee: Thomas Nelson, 2001.

Wacker, Grant. *Heaven Below*. Cambridge, Massachusetts and London, England: Harvard University Press, 2003.

Ward, Graham. *Christ and Culture*. Oxford: Blackwell Publishing, 2005.

Williams, Rowan. *On Christian Theology*. Oxford: Blackwell Publishing, 2000.

Wink, Walter. "Facing the Myth of Redemptive Violence." Ekklesia. May 21, 2012. No pages. Online: http://www.ekklesia.co.uk/content/cpt/article_060823wink.shtml.

Wood, Ellen Meiksins. *Empire of Capital*. London and New York: Verso, 2003.

Wright, N. T. *The New Testament and the People of God*. London: SPCK, 1997.

Subject/Name Index

Note: words such as church, empire, God, gospel, Jesus, politics, power, sovereignty and transcendence are so basic to the book's theme that they occur too frequently to be usefully included in this index.

A

Agamben, Giorgio, 30, 34, 56, 57, 63, 66, 81, 82, 90
America, 16, 18, 40, 58, 71–74, 78, 79, 87, 92, 95, 96
American Constitution, 59, 82, 95
Anabaptist, 48
Apostle Paul, 6, 14, 35, 45, 75
appeasement, 13, 21, 25, 27, 28, 42, 45, 53
Aquinas, Thomas. *See* Thomas Aquinas.
Aristotle, 34
atonement, 34, 43, 79
autonomy, 74, 81, 100–102, 104
Azusa Street, 67, 69, 72, 73

B

Badiou, Alain, 102
Bank of England, 37, 40, 53, 54, 94
Bartleman, Frank, 68–70
Benedict, 49
Bible, 69, 87, 89–91
biblical criticism, 88
biopower, 17, 18, 19, 61–63, 65, 85, 86, 102, 104
bishops, 9, 10, 24, 26
bourgeoisie, 39
Britain, 87, 92, 96
Burnet, Gilbert, 38, 40, 58, 94

C

Caesar
    Julius, 4
    Octavius, 4
    Tiberias, 4, 33
    Cult of, 66
capitalism, 17, 18, 28, 42, 52, 63, 74, 83
Catholic Church, 39, 67
Charlemagne, 32
Charles I, 55–57
Charles II, 39, 58
Christendom, 8, 32, 53, 65, 79